THE TRANSFORMATION SERIES
Gay Hendricks, *General Editor*

Books in The Transformation Series
explore the transitions of human life
and the possibilities
for happier, more creative living through the application
of the psychology of adjustment.

GAY HENDRICKS
is a professor at the University of Colorado and
a psychotherapist in private practice. His doctorate
in counseling psychology is from Stanford
University. He lectures and conducts workshops
in education and therapy both here and abroad.
Other books of his include *The Centering Book*
(with Russel Wills), *The Second Centering Book*
(with Tom Roberts) and *Transpersonal Education*
(with James Fadiman). Gay has a daughter named
Amanda and an English sheepdog named Millie.

CAROL LEAVENWORTH
is Director of the Career Counseling Center at
The Colorado College. She also maintains a private
practice in psychotherapy. She holds a master's
degree in counseling from the University of
Wisconsin. Carol's other activities include teaching,
lecturing, and being the mother of two children.

To Susan and Steven,
and to G.H.,
with love and gratitude
(C.J.L.)

To Amanda, as always,
and to the one
who made love real for me
(G.H.)

Contents

PREFACE

The purpose of this book is to present new ideas on living. By *living* we mean everything: communication, sex, relationships, money, work, parenting, and psychological and spiritual growth.

These are times of change and movement. Most people are looking for ways to live their lives more fully and creatively; they are opening up and becoming aware of their own hidden facets and potentials. Not too long ago, one had to move in rarified circles to hear words like self-actualization, growth, therapy, meditation. Now many people are following various paths to psychological and spiritual liberation. Books on meditation and Mexican Indian sorcerers occupy places on the best-seller lists right beside books about sex, power, cooking, and money.

The authors have written this book to assist those who are beginning to work on themselves as well as those who have been on growth paths for years. No matter where we begin or where we are, the basic processes of living are the same. Indeed, the experiences of the authors on their own paths, as well as their experiences with assisting others, have strengthened their conviction that whether or not people are deeply involved in personal growth, they all grapple with the same real-world problems: making relationships work, communicating caringly and effectively, and making friends with their sexuality, their minds, their bodies, and their feelings. For all of us, the parts of ourselves and our worlds that we neglect or deny become the very barriers in the way of our movement and growth.

Living is the thing we do most of, yet there is a shortage of clear information on how to do it. Much of the information that has come down from the classical religious teachings, while containing kernels of truth, has become tainted with dogma and doctrine that dilute its usefulness for people who are transcending belief and dogma in favor of a more creative, intuitive approach to living. Similarly, the truths drawn from our twentieth-century "religion," psychotherapy, are often difficult to extract from the jargon that accompanies each therapeutic system. One of the authors' main purposes in writing this book has been to present what we feel to be the very best information on living in as clear a manner as possible. In addition, the authors have evolved some new truths (or new ways of looking at very old truths), which we have used to liberate ourselves and our students and clients.

Today, many of us are asking fundamental questions about living:

- *Who am I?*
- *What am I doing here?*
- *How do I get more out of my relationships?*
- *How do I give, and get, more love?*
- *What is my relationship to the universe?*
- *How do I feel better (even if I'm not feeling bad)?*
- *How can I communicate who I really am to others?*

Questions like these are crucial; asking them makes us fully human. In fact, asking these questions, rather than accepting someone else's beliefs about them, is one of the most important things humans are doing at this point in evolution.

The authors are deeply interested in these issues for several reasons. First, we are always looking for more creative ways to live our own lives. Second, we are both therapists and teachers who are concerned with the welfare of our own clients and of the community at large. We are committed to giving away as much information on living as we possibly can. In additon, for reasons of economy of time (translatable as laziness), we want to put in writing the most essential messages we have been giving to others and using on ourselves over the years.

Every idea in the book has met two criteria. First, it has helped the authors live their own lives more effectively. Second, it has been used to help a wide variety of others to live and love more fully. In other words, there is nothing in the book that has not been tested by us, our friends, our clients, and our students in the most rigorous of laboratories—the real world. So, here is a guarantee: we will present no theories or philosophies, and we will ask you to accept no beliefs. We will write only about what works and what can be put to work in your own life. Indeed, if the ideas are put into practice, you will come to the end of the book with a radically different way of living your life. That is a strong claim, and we mean it.

All of us have everything we need to live our lives in beautiful, satisfying, flowing ways. Our problem is that we need a key or two to unlock our tremendous resources. You have everything you need, and you would probably discover everything in the book on your own sooner or later. If someone else had this information, however, the authors would want it in a concise form, so that is another reason for setting it down in writing.

So now you, the reader, know who the authors are, what the book is about, and why we have written it. We hope you will make a commitment to share the journey with us. From the people who have read and used the book before publication, several hints on reading it have emerged. First, it is all right to read it in small chunks. The ideas, although we have made them as clear as possible, reach into the deepest parts of ourselves, particularly those dark, dusty corners that we do not look into very often. When our conditioned ways of seeing the world are challenged, deep feelings are triggered, causing the mind to wander, shut down, spiral off, or rebel. One good way to handle this problem is to watch closely what your mind and body do as you read, so that reading the book becomes a process of awareness in itself. A third suggestion is to love and honor yourself for every reaction you have to the material (as well as to everything else in life). Gently, and with time, perhaps a lifetime away from the reading of this or any other book, all reactions may be replaced with love, making it possible for you to greet all of yourself, and all of life, as you would greet your beloved.

Gay Hendricks
Carol Leavenworth

1

THE PROBLEM

All of us experience difficulties from time to time in our daily lives. We may have conflicts with our children, our bosses, or our partners. We may become bored and dissatisfied with our lifestyles. We may worry about our ability to handle certain situations, to make effective decisions, or to meet our responsibilities. When problems arise, we may feel tense, anxious, angry, or depressed, and our minds become preoccupied with searching out a solution. Sometimes, finding no way to resolve the situation, we may decide that the best alternatives are either to resign ourselves to the condition or remove ourselves from it, perhaps by quitting a job, getting a divorce, or leaving town.

Usually, when we find ourselves in a difficult situation, we do not have a very clear understanding of how the problem came about. Other people do not seem to behave the way we would like them to: they may be critical when we want approval or cold when we need affection and understanding, defiant when we wish for compliance, or demanding when we want to be left alone. Often it seems that the more we do to get them to behave in the ways we would like, the more extreme becomes their tendency to behave in the opposite direction. A child who has been told to play quietly for awhile so as not to disturb an adult activity suddenly needs a drink, scrapes her knee, and breaks an ashtray—all in a half hour's time.

Some problems seem to occur repeatedly in one form or another. A husband and wife find that over the years their arguments have taken the same pattern, beginning and ending in the same ways. If they get a divorce and remarry, they may be dismayed to discover that they have similar conflicts with their new mates. A worker finds that the problems he or she experiences with a supervisor resemble problems that used to come up at school or at home. The supervisor seems to react very much the way parents or teachers did. The first tendency in such situations may be either to say, "Well, that's life" or "That's just how people are" or to become angry toward others and pessimistic about life in general. For each one of us, problems occasionally reach a point where we wonder, however briefly, if there is going to be any gain from persisting in an attempt to find a solution. At these times we may wonder if there is any reason for living.

It is just such situations and conflicts, confusing and painful as they may be, that provide each of us with the greatest and most challenging opportunities for growth. The most difficult problems we face are also the situations that provide us with the greatest chances to become more effective, more fully functioning, and happier human beings. Each one of us creates for himself or herself precisely and exactly the situations we need to move from confusion to clarity, from pain to peacefulness, and from helplessness to taking charge of our lives. And we will continue to create the same experiences again and again, with variations, until we take advantage of the opportunity and grow beyond it.

The first major barrier to perceiving our problems as an opportunity for growth comes from our beliefs. Each one of us is a storehouse of prejudice and opinion. We may believe that there is only one correct way to make a bed, that Roosevelt was either the greatest or the worst president that ever lived, or that the most important goal in a man's life should be to provide a high standard of living for his family. Our beliefs cause us to meet the challenges that life provides for us in rigid and stereotyped ways that do not allow for the creativity in thought and behavior that we need to unfold our potential for living fully and becoming more of what we truly are. Our uniqueness is stifled, and our ability to solve problems becomes limited.

Many of our beliefs originated in early childhood, from the words and actions of our parents and other important people. Our beliefs are also acquired from books, TV, and conclusions we have drawn from various experiences. Some of our beliefs were learned so thoroughly at such an early age and seem so "true" that we are not aware that they are merely beliefs and not necessarily valid. Less than a century ago people believed that if man had been meant to fly, he would have wings, and that a woman who revealed an ankle in public was an immoral person. Many of us today believe that it is important to sacrifice our own needs and wants to be loved and accepted, that real happiness is an impossible goal, or that it is necessary to struggle in order to achieve security. Because of these beliefs, we sacrifice, struggle, and attempt to accept our own discontent and disillusionment.

The authors have discovered that one of their major personal concerns is the same one shared by many of their clients and friends: how to live in close cooperation with others and get the love, attention, and caring we want. Sometimes love and attention come effortlessly while at other times—frequently just when we are feeling most needy and vulnerable—it seems difficult if not impossible to get what we need from others. Sometimes we blame a basic flaw in the other person, and at other times decide that personal relationships cannot work for us because we have some fundamental personality deficiency of our own that makes it impossible for us to live comfortably with other people. These conclusions were never satisfactory to us so we decided to look for other reasons for these situations to be occurring again and again in life.

Many of the problems we see within ourselves and others are reenactments of old issues or dramas in our lives rather than a result of the "way things are" or of other people's insensitivity or bad intent. Invariably we discover that our thoughts, feelings, and behavior in problem situations remind us of how we felt, thought, and behaved in other painful situations that occurred, perhaps many years previously. An argument that we may have had this week with a lover or a mate has many elements in common with conflicts we had years ago with Mom or Dad. Our feelings of anger and fear are the same ones we had at that time; our convictions of how the conflict will be resolved are based on how those previous conflicts ended; our behavior, whether we sulk or storm, give in or stubbornly hang on to our position, is just as it was then, perhaps with more complex and sophisticated variations.

The reenactment of old dramas is our personality's way of attempting to work out old situations that were not satisfactorily resolved for us when they originally arose.

Often, our beliefs, prejudices, and opinions insulate us from perceiving the potential for growth and creativity that is inherent in every problem confronting us. By hanging on to our beliefs, we maintain painful cycles of confusion and ineffective behavior in the face of the many opportunities for growth that our life presents to us. In order to break these cycles, it is first necessary to become aware of and to set aside our beliefs and to begin to examine our lives in the light of our own experience.

For example, Matt contacted one of the authors for therapy because he was experiencing an almost intolerable level of anxiety and mental confusion after his wife left him for another man. Matt was upset because in the past he had always been able to turn his back and walk away from similarly painful situations. He was concerned about both his state of mind and his lack of motivation to pull himself together and continue with his life.

When it was pointed out to him that he was attempting to short-circuit a normal grief reaction to the loss of an important person in his life, he responded by stating that he did not think it was appropriate for a man to experience or to express sadness. In further exploration, he identified the source of this belief. His father had never shown emotion and had taught his sons that the most important quality a man could possess was to meet every situation with a cool head and a rational outlook.

Matt eventually realized that he had attempted to disown a very important part of himself and that the pain he was experiencing over the loss of his relationship was intensified by his resistance to the normal grief and anger he could expect to feel in this situation. Additionally, he realized that his inability to feel and to express his feelings freely had led to the breakup in the first place.

Once Matt's beliefs about the appropriateness of experiencing and expressing feelings were identified and challenged, he was able to look at himself as he really was, rather than as he thought he must be. This change in perspective led to profound changes in Matt's experience of himself and ultimately in the quality of his life and relationships.

The first step, then, to achieving an effective and fulfilling life is to become aware of and begin to challenge the belief systems that limit our thinking and keep us trapped by our problems. Most people experience intense insecurity when they are asked to give up the "shoulds," "oughts," and "musts" in their lives. They worry that if they suspend beliefs they will become irresponsible and out of control and will surely hurt themselves and the people around them. They expect the social structure to crumble, resulting in personal and political chaos. This fear is understandable. When we let go of our limiting beliefs we jump off into the unknown, and the unknown is always scary. But beliefs are like a cocoon: they protect us while we need them, but we must discard them when we outgrow them.

In fact, when we lay aside our beliefs we find something deeper and stronger than externally imposed morality to guide us. We learn that our experiences, needs, and wants do not necessarily lead to destructive behavior. We become aware of the limitless alternatives available to us. We realize that our feelings and thoughts are cues to areas of potential growth and self-actualization. We become more rather than less responsible because we recognize that our behavior is something that only we control and that there are consequences to our behavior. The moment one assumes responsibility for his or her life, all compulsions fall away. We are left with our own experience and an unlimited opportunity to expand our real potential.

Everyone's journey toward inner peace and harmony with the outside world begins in the same place—who we are now at this point in our personal evolution. None of us is any more or less capable of living an effective and comfortable life than any other person. Happiness is not a goal but a way of being and perceiving. Our happiness is dependent on our willingness to use our ability to be in contact with ourselves and to accept the creative aspect of ourselves that recognizes every problem or negative situation as an opportunity to grow.

The techniques in the following chapters can be used any time, any place, any hour, any day. As you use the processes described here, you will discover your problems becoming more manageable. Situations that were once disturbing and frustrating will become simply challenging, like a puzzle to be put together. Boring tasks can be turned into experiments in self-discovery. Seemingly stagnant periods may be seen as opportunities for space and reflection. You will find your life's problems beginning to clear up just through looking at them and through tuning in to yourself and your needs and feelings.

2

WHAT WE DO THAT CAUSES THE PROBLEM

In the first chapter we saw how problems can be viewed as opportunities for growth, since they are tailor-made for us and therefore just what we need at the time they come up. This idea is sometimes difficult to accept. "My problems seem overwhelming," we may say. "What could be valuable about feelings like fear or pain?"

Pain is a forceful and dramatic attempt to get our attention. Just as the pain of an ulcer is an attempt by the body to draw attention to a breakdown in body function (and ultimately to get the person to consider changing the ulcer-producing lifestyle), so is the pain of a broken relationship an attempt to motivate us to find better ways of relating. Pain, then, is an opportunity to do something about it. Medicine has made great advances in treating physical pain; nearly everyone sees a physician for bodily aches and pains. Psychological pain is different because the treatments are exclusive (not available to all) and, in general, not as effective as treatments for physical pain. It is becoming common knowledge, however, that most visits to medical doctors are for illnesses of psychological origin.

How Psychological Problems Can Make Us Ill

Let us explore, for a moment, how psychological problems make us physically sick. Consider a man who is afraid, perhaps of losing his job or being left by his wife. Since males in our culture are not given much permission to feel scared, he may have been taught to deny his fear by thinking "I'm not afraid," at the first sign of scared feelings. Since he cannot accept these feelings, there is a lack of agreement between body and mind. The body is scared (tense shoulders, fast pulse), but the mind says, "No, I'm not." Since the mind has been conditioned so that it cannot accept *what is*, there is discontinuity between two important parts of his being. One of the common ways to cut off feeling is to tense one's muscles so that the sensations are not as intense. If this pattern continues—feelings: nonacceptance: tension—not only is the individual cutting himself off from an important part of his experience but also he is wasting a great deal of energy through tensing against feelings. If this tension persists, he may restrict the flow of blood and other life-energy systems to that area. If, for example, he chronically tenses his lower-back muscles in response to his scared feelings, he might weaken them to the point that picking up some object from the floor will result in back strain.

An example of an illness that is often psychologically induced is the common cold. Here is what happens. People often try to cut off feelings by restricting their breathing. Many of us have seen children who are scared or angry stop breathing for a moment. If a person is struggling with angry or hurt feelings and cannot accept these feelings or express them in a clear and nonthreatening way, he or she may restrict his or her breathing to keep from getting into the feeling deeply. Lessened air intake in the lungs, plus the tension in the area, may invite infection in the chest. Thus, the primary cause of the cold may be unaccepted hurt or anger, with the virus being a secondary cause.

How Do We Respond to Our Feelings?

How did we human beings get to be the way we are? How did we learn such inappropriate ways of handling our problems? Who taught us to ignore our feelings? How did we fail to learn to ask for what we want? For answers to these and other questions, we must look deeply into ourselves.

When we observe ourselves very carefully we make a penetrating discovery: our feelings occur at a deeper and more subtle level than our thoughts. For example, a woman may feel angry at her spouse. When this feeling reaches the level of thought, the thought may be in one of the following forms:

- *"He's no good."*
- *"Why did I marry him in the first place?"*
- *"I can never communicate with him."*
- *"I shouldn't be so angry."*

Although each of these thoughts has a slightly different meaning, they are all thought-level representations of the deeper feeling of anger.

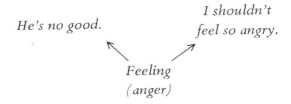

Each person responds to feelings in a different way. If three people are in a scary situation together, one might think, "I'm not afraid," another might think, "I've got to get out of here," while the third might think, "Why did I let them get me into this?" They would all be scared, but each would be dealing with the fear in a different way.

We often have a number of conflicting thoughts in response to a feeling. For example, a man might be frightened at learning that his wife is having an affair with another man. Some thoughts that might arise out of this fear are:

◻ *"It's okay—we're sophisticated."*

◻ *"I'll divorce her."*

◻ *"What about the children?"*

◻ *"I don't want to lose her."*

In the presence of deep feelings, our minds often respond with tremendously varied thoughts, until our minds seem "all a-jumble" with conflicting ideas. The crux of the problem is this: in such a situation we are both feeling and thinking, but we often do not acknowledge the feeling beneath all the thoughts. Rather, we attempt to select a plan of action from the jumble of information our mind is providing. Immediately we are faced with several problems. First, if we do not deal with the feeling we are experiencing, we are functioning without all the available information. Second, *all* of the thoughts that arise in response to a feeling are simply attempts by the mind to talk the body out of feeling. But the body *is* feeling, and any attempt to dissuade it from doing so will have one of two negative consequences. The most common consequence is that the mind keeps on trying to talk the body out of feeling, generating frustration and increased

stress. Another frequent consequence is that we train ourselves not to feel very deeply, in order to be able to talk
ourselves out of the feeling with little difficulty. As long as
we do not feel deeply, it is not difficult to deal with our
feelings. Unfortunately, inability to feel deeply may be the
biggest problem of all. When we lose contact with our feelings we cut off one of our most basic forms of experience.
Then our problems become very difficult to solve, because
we do not have access to the information we need. Solving
our problems without taking into consideration our feelings
is like trying to do arithmetic without the numbers. Where do
you begin?

At some point, usually very
early in our lives, we learn to talk ourselves out of feeling by
the application of thoughts that are "put in our heads" by
parents, teachers, and friends. For example, a child may feel
scared because of a bad dream. He may announce to his
sleepy parents that he is scared. Instead of helping him get
through the fear by giving him permission to feel it ('I'll bet
you feel scared"), his parents are likely to try to have him
turn off the fear by saying "There's nothing to be afraid of,"
or, "Don't be silly, there's no monster in your room." Gradually children internalize these injunctions so that later in life
when they feel scared, they say to themselves, "There's
nothing to be afraid of," rather than accepting their feelings
("I'm scared") and coming up with a plan to deal with them.
The ineffective style begins in denial and ends in confusion,
while the more effective technique begins in acceptance and
ends in action.

Unfelt Feelings
Cause Problems

When we leave behind unfelt feelings we create many trouble-some problems for ourselves. Unfelt feelings will not stay buried and later will come back to haunt us by influencing our feelings, our thoughts, and our actions.

Let's say we experience some anger in an interaction with a boss, but we do not take care of the anger at the time by deeply experiencing it, expressing it (if it's appropriate to do so), and letting it go. Unless we take care of our feelings in these ways (and other ways to be explained in chapter 4), we run the risk of having a backlog of feelings built up inside us. In this case, the unfelt and un-expressed anger may come back in the form of annoying thoughts ("Gee that guy's a creep. I wish I worked someplace else. I'm gonna look for another job. No, I like it here, the pay's pretty good, but I can't stand him. . . .").

Thoughts like these are the mental expression of the feelings trapped inside. Another way unfinished business in the feeling domain comes back to haunt us is in the form of physical tension. When we leave behind feelings in the body, our muscles have to tense in order to hold the feelings in. This results in the uncomfort-able feeling of overall tension many people experience.*

Possibly the most destructive aspect of unintegrated feelings, however, is the way they lead

*This phenomenon has also made Valium, a muscle-relaxing tran-quilizer, the best-selling drug in America.

us into repeating the same patterns of problem-causing situations over and over again. Even situations over which we may think we have little control are often the indirect result of feelings that we have ignored or denied. Here's how it works.

Abandoned feelings will seek expression in some way. We have seen how they express themselves in the form of nagging thoughts and physical tension. They also propel us into situations that call them forth, so that we can be given another opportunity to deal with them. If, for example, a person is carrying around a load of unintegrated anger, he will have the usual symptoms of irritating thoughts and muscle tension. He will also be creating situation after situation in which he can respond with anger. It is nature's way of giving us an opportunity to lighten our load of unintegrated feelings. It is the choice we are getting every minute to first embrace and then let go of those feelings with which we have been fighting and thus remaining attached to. If we can begin to see life this way, it can become a challenge rather than a curse, since we are always being given an opportunity to embrace what we have in the past ignored or denied.

There is another level to our understanding of feelings. Often, one feeling may be a cover for a deeper feeling. With men, the noisy feeling of anger frequently covers the quieter feeling of fear. A man may create anger-producing situations for himself only to find out, as his awareness grows, that fear is actually the deepest feeling he must work with. With women, often the quieter feelings like fear and sadness mask deeper feelings of anger. Both of these situations are the result of cultural conditioning. In our Western culture men are given permission to be angry but are not encouraged to accept and express fear and sadness, and the opposite is true for women. The problem is that *all* of us have *all* of the human feelings: anger, fear, sadness, joy, sexuality, excitement. To deny or ignore one or two or three of them is to become emotionally lopsided.

It takes much awareness to set up our lives in such a way that we create the opportunity to deal with unintegrated feelings. The patterns are often difficult to see because the feelings are buried very deeply. For example, Philip was abandoned by his mother at the age of six months, leaving him with deep feelings of anger and fear. He made the decision never to trust women. In his late thirties he was still acting out of his early experiences. He had had a dozen unsatisfactory relationships in which he experienced a lot of anger toward the women involved. He was suspicious and distrustful and often picked women who would meet his expectations of being untrustworthy and of leaving him.

Philip explained his problem as having bad luck with women. When he discovered the pattern, and the reasons for it, he quickly saw that luck played little part.

Thoughts and Feelings:
Is There a Difference?

Many people have asked whether there is any difference between thoughts and feelings. There is, and learning to tell the difference is one of the most enlightening experiences we can have. Here are some facts about feelings that may help us in our growth.

First, *all* feelings are *all* right. Feelings are the natural response of the body to various situations. It's what we do with those feelings that makes the difference. Lee Harvey Oswald was a man with a great deal of fear and anger bound up inside him. His fear and anger were appropriate responses to the chaotic upbringing he experienced. Had he learned to accept his anger and fear and express it appropriately, it might not have burst forth from him in the terrifying way it did. Feelings are OK; our problems arise when we set up internal battles through non-acceptance of them.

Feelings cannot be argued with. If you say to another person, "I'm angry with you," he cannot say, "No, you're not." However, if you communicate to him a thought or opinion that grows out of a feeling such as, "You're a jerk," he *can* say, "No, I'm not," and rightfully so. Some people try to dress up a thought or opinion by putting the phrase "I feel" before it, as if adding the term gives the opinion a depth or conviction (e.g., "I feel that you're a jerk."). This is easy to spot, because real feelings can usually be expressed in words of one or two syllables.

- *"I feel mad."*
- *"I'm scared."*
- *"I'm sad."*
- *"I'm feeling happy."*
- *"I'm excited."*

On the other hand, thoughts, beliefs, and opinions *need* extra words, and as we said before, they can be argued about. So, if someone says, "My gut feeling is that Joe is a clod," that is a thought, not a feeling. The feeling beneath such a statement is, "I'm angry with Joe," or, "I'm scared of Joe." Many human interactions can be clarified by going from the relative level of opinion and belief to the absolute level of feelings, so careful attention to the communication of feelings is highly recommended. The later chapter on communication is all about how to do this.

Our problems begin when there is disunity within us, particularly of thought and feeling. Feelings are happening all the time, but we often ignore or deny them by covering them with a protective veneer of belief and opinion. When we are out of touch with our feelings and our needs, it is not possible to live effectively.

3

GETTING OUT FROM UNDER THE PAST

Many of our feelings are perfectly reasonable responses to real things that are happening in our lives. All of us experience some degree of anxiety when confronted by a new situation such as a job interview or speaking in public for the first time. The grief (and anger) we feel when saying goodbye to good friends or at the loss of someone or something very important to us is real and appropriate. While these feelings can be intense and painful, they make sense to us, and if we allow ourselves to experience them fully, they will eventually become integrated and pass from our lives.

Other feelings we have are in many ways more troublesome and confusing to us because, while they are often (but not always) related to our current experience, they are actually replays of old unintegrated feelings from months, years, even decades, in the past.

Learning to differentiate between old, or archaic, feelings and feelings arising directly from here and now experiences can sometimes be helpful with the integration process and in interpersonal and situational problem solving. Problems that seem to come up repeatedly often arise out of old unintegrated feelings. If you find yourself thinking, "Here we go again," or, "Why does this always happen to me?" you have a clue to an old problem. Also, sometimes you may observe yourself reacting with feelings that are out of proportion to the actual situation or, on reflection, feel that you may have overreacted to a comment or some occurrence. This may indicate archaic feelings rising to the surface.

All of us have experienced a feeling of anxiety, tension, or depression that persistently troubles us even in times when we would normally be feeling good. Sometimes it seems that the feeling could be related to many things in our present lives but not clearly to any one event or problem. The tendency is to pass things off ("one of those down days") or attach the feeling to some convenient event such as the onset of menstruation or a later-than-usual bedtime. While these events may be related to or intensify the feeling, they are usually not the *cause* of it. Looking beyond the surface in such instances often reveals an old fear, anger, or sadness seeking recognition.

Sometimes we have feelings that seem to continually get in the way of effective action. We may find that our feelings seriously undermine or totally subvert successful handling of a situation. That is a clue to an archaic problem interfering in the present. You may find that it seems as if every time you sit down to discuss a certain problem with a boss, mate, or friend you end up feeling frustrated or angry. Or even after making many public presentations, you still feel intensely uncomfortable or anxious. If so, the *cause* of the feeling lies somewhere else than in the here and now situation. Fear of flying, fear of high places, fear of being enclosed in small spaces, and other phobias of this nature are not generally caused by the danger implicit in the situation itself, but are leftover feelings from the past that may cause us more or less inconvenience depending on our individual lifestyle. A capable and intelligent woman had a great deal of difficulty landing a job because her fear of tests severely impeded her performance on test batteries given by most personnel departments. After one session of therapy in which she integrated this fear, she found a job within a week.

Sometimes a problem or a person with whom we are having difficulty reminds us of situations or people in our past. Often our intimate partners seem similar to one of our parents. We can deal simultaneously with the present concern and its archaic component. A man, feeling irritated at his wife for reminding him to carry an umbrella, can ask her to stop doing that and also can relate that feeling to an old feeling of irritation or anger toward his overprotective mother.

Feelings Are
Signposts toward Growth

All the feelings we experience are signposts pointing the way toward growth and greater realization of our own potential as human beings. Some feelings are clear and bold. Their message is readily apparent. Others present themselves less clearly, and their message may require some effort to decipher. Feelings such as guilt, frustration, hurt, resentment, disappointment, depression, and longing generally are a mask for more straightforward feelings of anger, fear, sadness, or excitement. Thoughts comparing a present situation with something in the past or with fantasies of future delights can tell us something about who we are and often can also cover unintegrated feelings of joy. Feelings and thoughts that mask more direct and powerful feeling states are often clues to feelings from the past that we have not allowed ourselves to totally experience. The guilt and uneasiness we may feel at having made a mistake in judgment or a social faux pas may bring to mind the fear we felt as a child upon breaking a favorite ashtray or trinket. One of the authors (C.L.) experiences a recurring fantasy of living in a cottage by the ocean. Over the years, this fantasy has been elaborated to include many small details of the surroundings and the activities she would engage in there. At one point she was convinced that she would be a different person, more whole, joyful, and peaceful, if only she were living in such a place. Looking at this, she realized that the fantasy came from the many happy and pleasurable feelings she had as a child living near Puget Sound, particularly the excitement she felt on stormy days when the waves crashed against the beach.

Sometimes we experience such intense feelings that we are afraid that if we were to give in to them they would consume us, and we would never be able to give them up. This situation occurs most often in periods of high stress. A feeling of anger that seems endless or a bottomless sorrow is a mask for a more direct feeling. A feeling of endless anger, for example, may cover an old fear that, once exposed, can be used to provide precisely the growth experience needed at that moment in life.

Harry, whose wife had decided that her needs were not being met within their relationship and was making plans to separate from him, experienced such intense anger that he was convinced of the necessity of placing strict controls on his feelings in order not to hurt her or someone else physically. After allowing himself to experience the anger in a safe and protected situation, he realized that underlying the anger was an intense fear of abandonment, related to times in his childhood when he would wake up crying from a nightmare and no one would come to him.

Clara, who felt depressed and was worried by her increasing tendency to withdraw, particularly from men she cared for, controlled the tears she felt rising to the surface each time she thought about her problems. Succumbing to those tears, she felt, would put her into a bottomless depression, a crying jag from which she would never return. Looking more closely at those sad feelings, which she labeled as "being sorry for myself" and for which she severely criticized herself, she realized that they covered a deep anger toward both her former husband and her father that she had never allowed herself to feel or express at the times when it would have been appropriate to do so.

Children's Uninhibited Feelings

Children are born a bundle of needs and feelings. Each time a baby experiences a need she lets us know in very direct ways until the need is met. Similarly, small children gurgle, coo, bubble, wave their arms, smile, and laugh when they feel excited or happy. Some of what psychologists call a child's short attention span, at least in very small children, can possibly be attributed to their directness in seeking gratification for their wants and needs and their ability to fully integrate their feelings about each situation quickly and naturally. Small children experience their feelings very clearly. Fear, anger, sadness, joy, and excitement are clearly communicated even though the children do not have the verbal skills to label them as such. Their emotions are written all over their bodies and faces, because as yet they have not been "socialized" to control their feelings and confuse themselves about whether it is good or bad to feel. They simply do feel, and they do it with the entirety of their personhood.

At some point early in our development, each one of us came to a startling realization. We learned that our needs would not automatically and magically be met, that we were dependent on large and powerful beings for our very survival. As we grew, we found that these people, our parents and others in charge of our care, were less and less interested in doing everything we wished them to do. We were actually going to be required to feed ourselves, put on our own clothing, and tie our own shoes when we would much rather be playing in the sand or exploring an ant hill. Not only that, there were things called rules that we had to follow. If we did not follow them big people became angry and sometimes spanked or put us in a room by ourselves. These facts were very scary and confusing to us. We began to try to figure out ways to keep important people in our lives happy with us so we would continue to get the love, attention, and protection we needed. At this point moms and dads and all kinds of other people were giving us messages about what we could do, what we should do, think, and feel, how we should behave, and what was wrong with us. And we listened, because we believed that if we did not we would not be able to survive. Also, we probably decided that they were right, because they were big, powerful, and seemed as if they knew everything and could do anything.

The problem that begins here and persists all through our lives is this: parents and others do not know the importance of fully feeling our feelings before we go on to solving the problems before us. Parents are scared by the intensity of their children's feelings and also by the possibility that the children will grow up to be "uncivilized" or bad reflections on the parents and their parenting skills. Sometimes parents are tired or preoccupied with their own problems and do not have the energy to deal with their children.

The result is that the world around us does not encourage us to have the full experience of our emotions. If a child has a nightmare and comes to the parent for comfort, the response very often is, "It's only a dream. There's nothing to be afraid of. Go back to bed." A very real feeling of fear has been minimized. In fact the child has been told that her feeling is not even real or appropriate, and she may repeat to herself, "There's nothing to be afraid of; there's nothing to be afraid of," thereby participating in the minimization of the importance of feeling and beginning to learn "self-control."

Children are often told when feeling angry about some conflict with a playmate, "Big boys don't cry," or even more directly, "It doesn't do any good to get angry." The message is clear: stop feeling your angry feelings. The child may also sense the parent's own discomfort with expressions of anger and decide that he had better be less expressive to keep Mom's or Dad's approval and caring.

In Marion's family an overlay of peacefulness covered a very stressful situation. No one ever raised his or her voice, especially not in front of the children. Angry feelings were rarely named, and verbal expressions of anger did not exist. Once when she was seven or eight Marion became quite angry at not being allowed to do something she wanted to do and began kicking the leg of an old chair. Immediately she was instructed not to kick furniture, but no other alternatives were suggested to deal with the feeling, and her last outlet for expressing anger was closed off to her. It was many years before Marion became aware of feeling angry again, and when she did, she was astonished at the amount of energy she expended to keep such feelings below the level of awareness.

When we are sad we are told that it will be better tomorrow. The underlying message is, "Forget it. Don't pay attention to it, and it will go away." "Keep a stiff upper lip" and "Stop feeling sorry for yourself" continue to be popular clichés meant to control sad feelings. Most of us don't know how to deal with grief or sadness and therefore admire to the point of idolatry such public displays of control as the former Jacqueline Kennedy's widely televised performance at the death of her husband, John. The lesson we learn is that if people are going to be sad it shouldn't last too long and should only be done privately. We learn this lesson quite well as children and struggle to master the technique of holding back our tears.

Even feelings of joy and excitement, we learn, are necessary to control. How many times did big people tell us to calm down or not to get so excited? As each natural feeling bubbled up to the surface to be expressed we were told again and again to calm down, control, forget, and minimize until we not only stopped expressing much feeling but in many situations actually stopped being aware that we felt at all. We learned to pay no attention to the messages our body sent us and to talk ourselves out of expressing those that we did get in touch with.

In addition, before we ourselves can put proper and appropriate names to our feelings, parents often confuse the issue further by redefining our feelings in terms that they are more comfortable with. A child who is appropriately afraid of an unfamiliar person in the household will hear Mom or Dad say, "Oh, he's just shy." Thinking it over, the child decides he must be shy if the parent says so and proceeds to define many feelings of fear as shyness.

When Jody was in eighth grade and going to her first formal dance, her very appropriate terror in face of this strange situation was defined as excitement by her mother. As a result of that and many other similar experiences, Jody still has some difficulty in distinguishing between the two feelings.

The consequence of the messages we have received from parents and other important sources is that we learn that the way to please others and to get along in the world is to control, minimize, deny, and redefine our feelings. We do not learn to feel fully or to express feelings appropriately. Instead, we learn the rules for our behavior in the world, for relating to peers and authority figures, and for dealing with social situations. In other words, we learn "programs" for our behavior. A program is a more or less ritualized set of thoughts, feelings, and actions that we apply fairly automatically to events occurring in our daily lives. If someone bumps into us in a crowded store we may *think* an angry thought such as, "I wish he'd watch where he's going," *feel* irritated, but *say,* "Excuse me." Some of the programs we've learned are positive and helpful in that they keep us out of jail and mental institutions and help us move through the world with a minimum of hassle. An example is the program that tells us to watch traffic when we cross the street. Although many of our programs neither help nor hinder us to any great extent, some are quite negative in their effect and cause us more problems than solutions. An example is the program that tells us, "People can't be trusted." All programs narrow our alternatives for behavior and expression and limit our ability to act in spontaneous and creative ways.

Programs are based on old unintegrated feelings. Since we did not learn to feel our feelings fully, to express feelings appropriately, or to solve problems and take action taking our feelings into consideration, we needed to learn other ways of dealing with situations in which we felt certain feelings. One very common program that most children develop during the early school years is the "fairness" program. This program arises out of unintegrated feelings of fear and anger over the realization that no matter how much the child wants something, others may not be willing to give it to him or her. The essential proposition of the fairness program is that if I can't have everything I want, neither can you. All parties involved agree to go along with "what's fair" in order to get at least part of what they want in the situation. Problems arise when there are disagreements about what is fair in the situation or when one party gets what he or she wants and doesn't provide the other with what was agreed upon in return. Grownups who automatically apply fairness programs to problem situations can be cutting themselves off from an opportunity to know themselves better and to find more creative solutions to problems than compromise generally provides. To check yourself for a fairness program, see if you look for the fair solution, if you wonder if others are being fair to you, or if you find yourself blaming or judging others for their lack of fairness.

Old Programs
Die Hard

Old programs are very much a part of us in many ways. They affect our way of viewing the world, color our perceptions of the behavior of others, and determine much of our day-to-day behavior and our expectations of ourselves, of others, and of life. Programs are a part of our thoughts, attitudes, and values. They can create conflict both within ourselves and with others.

Generally, the older a program is, the more difficult it is to identify and the more unavailable the original feeling is to our everyday awareness. There are some common programs that affect most of us to some extent. These programs are based on very old, very deep feelings like:

□ *fear of being abandoned*

□ *fear of losing parents' love or care*

□ *anger and fear about feeling powerless*

□ *fear of our sexuality*

□ *fear of death*

These are all common childhood feelings based on the child's perception of the world. They are a normal part of the growing-up process. They only form the basis for troublesome programs in adult life when they remain unrecognized and unintegrated.

Fear of abandonment or loss of love, when unintegrated, leads to programs meant to control the actions and/or feelings of others. Instead of experiencing the fear in situations that call up this program, we may use reasoning, power plays, manipulation, or anger to keep the situation under control. When John and Alice agreed to an "open marriage" contract they expected to have some adjustment problems. Being intelligent adults with a positive and long-standing relationship, they felt that they could handle anything that came up by keeping lines of communication open and discussing problems as they arose. They had not, however, taken into consideration John's old abandonment fears. John had been orphaned at an early age and spent most of his childhood in a series of foster homes. Each time he began to form a close attachment to his foster parents, he was uprooted. John was not aware that part of his desire for an open marriage came out of old fears of becoming too dependent on another person for love and closeness. Nor did he forsee that the new marriage agreement would call out the unintegrated feelings he had about this insecure childhood.

After some experimentation with outside relationships, John found himself so uncomfortable with the situation that he wanted a return to the old "closed" marriage. Alice was not so sure. John tried reasoning with her to no avail. No matter how convincing his arguments and theories supporting a return to their old life style, Alice preferred the open contract. Next he tried therapy, hoping to get some solutions and also hoping that Alice, a counseling student, would find him more interesting if he could talk her language. Later he alternated between periods of withdrawing his attention from her and angry confrontations in which he threatened to leave the country and to cut Alice off from contact with her children and financial support. Threats, promises, and persuasion were not effective in altering Alice's behavior, nor were they helpful to John who only found himself more frustrated and unhappy as time went on. Not only could he not control Alice's feelings, wishes, and behavior, but eventually through his attempts to do so, he created just the situation he most feared—the loss of Alice's affection and good will. Had he recognized and integrated his abandonment fear earlier, he might have saved his marriage and been able to find a satisfactory solution to his problem of insecurity.

Similarly, fears and angers felt as a child about our helplessness with respect to grownups' wishes and demands and our inability to meet grownups' expectations can cause us to behave toward bosses and other authority figures in ways that are detrimental to our success and effectiveness in these relationships. Common examples are the rebellious worker and the yes man. Other programs can be more subtle. Sue was a competent and effective worker, with the ability to define problems and come up with solid solutions. Working with a boss who respected and praised her good work, Sue enjoyed her job and had plenty of time for herself and her family. But when she moved to a new job where expectations were not clearly defined, Sue experienced a great deal of stress. Even after she came up with reasonable standards by which to measure her own performance, the problem did not diminish. Those in authority questioned her decisions and were not supportive of her as her previous boss had been. Sue continued to experience a good deal of anxiety and began to drive herself to meet all the expectations and needs of boss, clients, and the staff she supervised. She had little time to meet her personal needs, felt overwhelmed by responsibility, and eventually became ill enough to go to bed. In reviewing what had happened, Sue realized that her compulsion to push herself beyond reasonable limits was a result of her unintegrated fear and anger about her parents' unrealistic expectations of her and the lack of praise she received as a child.

Habitually blaming others for our difficulties is a result of old fears and angers about having to take responsibility for ourselves as we are growing up. Most of us have serious doubts about our ability to get our needs met and to get what we want on our own. It is hard to face up to the fact that the negative things that happen in our lives are our responsibility alone if we are carrying around old feelings about our ability to cope with life's difficulties. It is much more comfortable to blame others when troubles arise. The typical case of separation and divorce is a striking example. In marriage breakups, most individuals focus on the faults of the other party, placing the blame on the shoulders of the other without looking for their own part in the conflicts that led to the separation.

Toby and Joe fell in love when they were both in their teens. Neither of them was aware of the insecurities they were trying to resolve within their marriage. Toby believed at a deep level that she was unlovable and needed constant evidence of Joe's affection to feel adequate. Joe had never learned to express his deeper feelings and also wanted to be protected from situations where he would be expected to express himself in ways that he could not handle. When conflict arose in the relationship, neither Toby nor Joe was strong enough to discuss their problems and still maintain their own feelings of adequacy. Their relationship was characterized by long periods of false peace that would periodically erupt into violent arguments. After thirty years of marriage, they separated, each one blaming the other for the failure of the relationship. They lived apart for many years, but although they were never able to achieve a reconciliation, neither could they begin divorce proceedings. Neither Toby nor Joe ever gained the personal strength needed to bring closure to the situation. They both needed to integrate the old feelings that were the basis of their inability to share and solve problems, but they never succeeded in doing so.

Other common programs arise from fears and anxiety about sexual feelings. The simplest examples of such programs are believing that men are after only one thing, or that all women need is a "good lay." In many cases, such problems as inability to achieve sexual satisfaction and worry that our bodies are unattractive arise out of old programs.

Nancy visited a therapist because of her belief that she was frigid and her concern that this would lead to the breakup of her marriage. She quickly learned that her problem was not frigidity. Instead, she found that she did not allow herself to experience the *feeling* of being sexually aroused. When she had an orgasm through masturbation, she reached climax very quickly and many times was not sure quite what had happened. The homework that the therapist gave her to do alone and with her husband left her emotionally cold, although she lubricated and also overcame a tendency to constrict her vagina, thereby making penetration difficult.

In exploring the basis of her fear of letting go and feeling sexy, Nancy recalled overhearing her father and mother arguing about sex when Nancy was only five or six. She remembered her father shouting, "Only whores want a man to do that to them," and leaving the house. Nancy discussed with the therapist the fear she had felt at the time of the incident as well as the fear she felt in later years whenever she found herself getting sexually aroused. Over a period of several weeks she worked at integrating those fears. Soon she was able to allow herself to experience increasing sexual pleasure both through masturbation and lovemaking with her husband.

Old programs are reflected in our bodies as well as in our feelings and behavior. As we learn, during childhood, to control our feelings, we tense certain muscles in our bodies in order to stop ourselves from acting on a feeling and to cut off awareness of the feeling. A child who hunches his or her shoulders in fear of a parent's anger will have a tendency to hunch in other fear-producing situations. As an adult he or she may have permanently raised shoulders, held in place by chronic muscle tension in that area. This person literally cannot relax and lives constantly with fear. But only particularly stressful situations bring this tension to the surface, and then the clue may be a stiff neck or shoulder pain. Headaches, chronic stomach tension, high blood pressure, ulcers, chronic bronchitis or asthma, and muscle tics are just a few other clues to unintegrated feelings stored in the body.

Old fears, angers, sadnesses, and joys come up in our everyday life in our feelings, thoughts, and behaviors. Problems that we can't seem to solve no matter how hard we try and situations that recur or in which our feelings seem to be repeating a familiar pattern give us the clues we need to look for an old program. Our ordinary responses—including changing the subject, withdrawing from the situation, or blaming others for our difficulty—only insure that the program will recur in a different form. When we know how to solve a problem and then do so, or when we are clear as to what additional information we need to solve the problem, we are operating in a program-free situation. If we did not have old programs we would be able to solve all our problems without significant emotional effort or pain.

Each painful situation that arises, rather than being something to avoid, curse, or turn away from is actually an opportunity for growth, which if embraced totally, would yield the joy that arises from freedom to control our own lives. Since the only way to get over a feeling is to go through it, old programs are given up and real growth achieved only through the integration of the feelings that support the program.

Feelings resulting from archaic programs are the most difficult to integrate because they are hard to recognize at first and because they have been with us for such a long time that they seem to be a very real and reasonable part of our personalities. With practice, it becomes easier and easier to identify and integrate old feelings. Often, when we begin to be aware of the feelings underlying our programs we fear that if we once tap into a feeling it will overwhelm us and we will lose control or go crazy. The truth is that experiencing our feelings cannot destroy us. Our emotional experience is a beautiful part of our humanness, and by allowing ourselves to feel our feelings, we experience ourselves as more whole and together rather than less so. Closing off of feeling is the truly self-destructive behavior because then we cut ourselves off from the inner core of our person-hood, and we can literally destroy our bodies and our important relationships.

Even in a therapeutic situation it is rare for an old feeling to be integrated through a single experience. A feeling is integrated over a period of weeks and months by acknowledging and experiencing it as completely as we can whenever it comes up in our lives. Each time we repeat this process with love for ourselves and our feelings, the old program loses some of its power to control our behavior and thoughts. Every time we integrate a feeling we gain a little more control over our own lives until, finally, the old feeling leaves us entirely.

4

HOW TO WATCH YOUR PROBLEMS SOLVE THEMSELVES

Up until the time of Copernicus, the established view was that the stars and the sun revolved around the earth. This view was supported by scientists, laymen, and, above all, by the church. Basing their assumptions on this "obvious fact," astronomers developed tremendously complicated theories to account for the movement of the planets. The more complicated the theories became, however, the less astronomers were able to understand the movement of the planets. The history of astronomy is full of people who spent their lives working out more and more complicated explanations based on one major misconception.

In many ways, living is like that ancient study of the solar system. If we begin with the wrong assumptions, life can become unnecessarily complicated and consistently unsatisfying. Since living often seems so complicated, could there be one thing we are doing wrong at the base of it all? And if we were to alter that one thing, could we smooth out our lives? It is the conviction of the authors that there is one such thing that we are doing wrong.

The Core and
How to Get There

Feelings are the undercurrent of everything we do. Unintegrated feelings get in the way of seeing things as they really are. The feelings that are most troublesome are unintegrated ones from the past. As became clear in the last chapter, these archaic feelings cause our present actions to come from an out-of-date base.

What are some clues we can use to let us know when we need to integrate a feeling? One of the best ways to tell that unintegrated feelings are in the air is to watch thoughts. For example, when we have recurring thoughts of a past situation (for instance, an argument or a death in the family), it often means that certain feelings are trying to get our attention. Similarly, having a number of fantasies about the future, either positive or negative, means that there is some fear or anxiety we need to integrate. (If you're wondering how to integrate a feeling, you're only a page or two away from a discussion of just that.) When we find ourselves talking to ourselves in our own voice (what we will call self-talk), it often means that there is a feeling underneath that needs to be integrated. So, there are three major mental symptoms of unintegrated feelings.

Feelings are deep and subtle entities; it takes much observation to be able to detect them as they occur. Nature, however, gives us a number of very visible signs when feelings need to be dealt with. One of these visible signs is thought—the memories, fantasies, and self-talk discussed above. Another clear indication that feelings are trying to get our attention is body tension. At the moment a feeling occurs, it manifests itself simultaneously in the body in several ways. Often, there is muscle tension. Most of us have experienced a tight stomach or a tense neck; these are two of the ways the body signals us that feelings need to be integrated. Another way that feelings affect the body is by turning on the autonomic nervous system, which is the system that makes the palms sweat and the heart beat faster. Scientists call such reactions the "fight or flight" syndrome, because it is thought that our cave-dwelling ancestors used them to survive in a hostile environment. Now, of course, our dangers are more psychological than physical, but we still have the fight or flight equipment built into our bodies.

Another clue that we have unintegrated feelings is ineffective behavior. If our best intentions keep on failing, if we keep engaging in repetitive actions that seem to get us nowhere, it is often because we are acting out of unintegrated feelings. When we are in thrall to archaic feelings, our present actions will seem ineffective, because we are not responding to the current situation. To illustrate, one of the authors' clients talked about acting surly toward the cashier where he usually ate lunch. We asked, "Who does she look like?" He paused for a moment, then grinned sheepishly. "Mom," he said. His old feelings of anger toward his mother did not fit the current situation.

Doing It

There is a simple procedure to use when dealing with feelings. It is the key to mental health, and the authors strongly encourage you to internalize it so that it becomes a way of life. It works.

In general, the procedure involves giving ourselves full permission to have every reaction we have, and to love ourselves for all our reactions to things. Here's how it goes.

Waking Up

The first thing that needs to be done is to observe a thought, an action, or a bodily sensation that you think may be connected to a feeling. Mary talked about being upset because she was snubbed by someone. She thought, "He can't hurt me, I'm strong." This thought is a defense against the deeper feeling of anger or fear. In the same situation, a more aggressive person might have a flushed face or pound a fist into a hand. All of these cues are helpful to us because they provide us with the passageway down into the feelings beneath. Instead of hating ourselves for our ineffective behavior and thoughts and our body tension, we can begin to see these manifestations as our best friends, since they are the cues that give us the opportunity to get deeper into ourselves.

Harmonizing the Mind

After the cue has been observed, the next step is to harmonize the mind by trying on a mental feeling-statement. Following the observation of a thought like the above, "He can't hurt me . . .," we might try a feeling-statement like "I'm scared."

The three basic feeling-statements that have been found to be most useful are:

◻ *"I'm scared."* . . .

◻ *"I'm angry."* . . .

◻ *"I'm sad."* . . .

It's tremendously liberating to make a simple statement of feeling like "I'm scared." It is helpful, though not essential, to complete the feeling-statement by saying why we are feeling that way. In the above example, it might be "I'm scared because I don't want to be hurt." Making a mental feeling-statement is liberating because it lines us up with what is, harmonizing our conscious mind with what is going on beneath it, on the feeling level. When we are feeling one thing (like fear) but thinking something else (like "Nothing can scare me"), we are out of alignment with ourselves. Like

a car with wheels out of alignment, we wobble. People notice, perhaps only on a subconscious level, that we are not
balanced and centered. Another important reason to make
feeling-statements is that when we do we are taking responsibility for our feelings and thereby beginning to take charge
of our lives. Most of us have been trained by parents, teachers, and society to be powerless and to blame others for our
feelings. When we take a victim stance in the world, we
surrender our power. One way we give up our power is by
thinking that others "cause" our feelings. When we make a
feeling statement like "I'm angry," we are taking full responsibility for our anger, rather than saying " ___ made me
angry." The same principle holds for fear and sadness as well
as for positive feelings such as happiness, excitement, and
sexual sensation. Feeling-statements like "I'm happy . . .,"
"I'm excited . . .," and "I'm sexually attracted to . . ." are
essential also, because they give our bodies permission to feel
positive feelings.

The next step is to let our-
selves feel the feeling as deeply as we can. This is a physical
step because it involves giving ourselves totally over to the
feeling for a moment. Some people like to take a deep breath
and imagine sending the fear all the way to their toes. Others
develop a sense of "giving in" to the feeling and letting the
fear, sadness, or anger wash over them for a moment. This
step is important. We have seen how half-felt feelings create
unfinished business that comes back to haunt us. By letting
ourselves feel as deeply as we can, we clean up old business
and prevent further unfinished business from accruing.

People have wondered if this procedure leads people to wallow in their feelings. The answer is no; the exact opposite is true. When people wallow in their feelings, it is because they are not giving themselves permission to feel the feeling deeply. Another reason is that they haven't found the deepest feeling to integrate. For example, we may see people who "cry at the drop of a hat." Perhaps that's because they are not experiencing their sadness deeply enough to let it go. Or, the sadness may be drawing their attention to a deeper feeling, perhaps anger or fear. If a feeling recurs, either it has not been felt deeply enough or it is a cover for a deeper feeling.

Next, it is important to love ourselves for feeling whatever it is that we are feeling. Whatever it is, is what needs to be felt. Resistance to it has kept it trapped inside us. When we resist sexual feelings, for example, they do not go away. Rather, they come back stronger or in roundabout ways like fantasies and sexual games (such as flirting, innuendoes, dirty jokes). The classic old maid who sees everyone as sexually obsessed is doing so because she is resisting her own sexual feelings and needs. Because the brakes are on her own feelings very tightly, she must act her feelings out in warped ways. The same thing is true for fear and anger. When we resist anger, we run into situation after situation that makes us angry. When we resist fear, we live scared.

To resist something is to let it run our life. When we can drop our resistance, let ourselves feel whatever it is, and give ourselves love for feeling it, we

make friends with the part of ourselves that has been neg-
lected or denied. It is a tricky thing to do because we are
trained not to love and accept many parts of ourselves. We
may say, "I could never love myself for feeling *that*." The
paradox, of course, is that the feelings we have most trouble
loving are the ones that most desperately are trying to get us
to love them. The feelings that inhabit the murky depths of
each of us are those that most need to be lovingly brought to
the surface.

A glance through the authors'
files reveals some of the feelings with which normal people
struggle:

◻ *hatred for a brother or sister*

◻ *fear of being abandoned*

◻ *sexual attraction for a parent*

◻ *fear of being ridiculed*

◻ *grief over a loss*

With feelings, the way out is always through. In other words,
the feeling is dissolved by experiencing it deeply and by sur-
rounding it with love until all resistance is overcome. What
gets us stuck is withdrawing our awareness from a feeling;
freedom comes from dropping the resistance and bathing the
feeling in awareness.

Love is one of the tools of our
salvation. If we can lovingly accept ourselves, *everything*

about ourselves, we have resolved all conflicts within us. If we then can extend that love to others, loving them just the way they are, we have resolved all conflicts between ourselves and the rest of the world. The first step, though, is to love ourselves for everything we feel. If we have feelings that we think are hostile, immoral, or childish, then we need to love ourselves for feeling just that way. One of the lovely paradoxes of life is that the only way to rid ourselves of an unwanted feeling is to love ourselves for having it. If this is hard to understand, love yourself for feeling confused.

In loving ourselves, we always start where we are. Since most of us have many parts of ourselves we do not like very much, we must usually start by loving ourselves for not loving ourselves. When we have loved our resistance, when we have given ourselves total, loving permission to hate ourselves, the space opens for us to love ourselves even more. If this process seems difficult, love yourself for making it difficult, for not understanding, for whatever your experience is. Whatever *is* is what needs to be loved.*

Whenever we observe a thought, an action, or a physical tension, and use it as a cue to dive down to the feeling level beneath, we are taking a journey to the very core of our being. We are leaving the

*Readers will enjoy *The Lazy Man's Guide to Enlightenment* by Thaddeus Golas (Palo Alto, California: The Seed Center, 1971). It is a perfect jewel of a book that explores deeply the concept of loving yourself.

world of illusion and conditioning, and plunging down into what actually *is*. This plunge is the central creative movement in life, because the experience of *what is* opens the space for the creative flow of the universe to speak through us.

The creative plunge may be taken hundreds of times a day, hundreds of thousands of times in a lifetime. Taking it gives our lives excitement and gives us confidence that we are in step with the universe. After taking the plunge, it is useful to return to the surface with our energy coalesced around the will, so that our actions have direction and purpose. Therefore, a final step is to determine what you want. After letting yourself feel the feeling deeply, figure out what you want and/or need by making an "I want" or "I need" statement in your mind. For example, after giving herself permission to feel fear that her husband might have a relationship with another woman, a woman said, "I want an agreement from him that says he won't do that without discussing it with me and a third party." Here are several other examples:

- *"I'm scared of being alone"* and *"I want someone to hold me for a while."*

- *"I'm sad about my children's being away at camp"* and *"I want some constructive ways of filling the time I usually spend with them."*

- *"I'm sexually attracted to Jim"* and *"I want to know if he's attracted to me."*

⊏ *"I'm angry at Sue for yelling at me"* and *"I want her assurance that she will think about why she does that so much."*

In phrasing wants and needs, it's important not to edit them very much, particularly at first. Most of us have been so conditioned not to think about what we want or need that to do so is very difficult. We place many barriers in our way such as thinking that our wants are silly or selfish. In fact, many of our wants *are* silly and selfish when we view them through our adult eyes, but it's important to give ourselves permission to be aware of them because they may come from an early time in our lives when we did not get something we wanted or needed. Among the things people need beyond the physical are love, a feeling of being valued, and positive attention. In our childhood people often were stingy with these kinds of things, giving us instead negative attention such as scolding, or plastic substitutes for love such as toys. As a result, many adults seem to set things up in such a way as to get exactly the opposite of what they need. We probably all know people who drive others away when they most need them. Similarly, those who have been trained to accept plastic substitutes for love find that in adult life they want material possessions (but are never quite satisfied with what they have).

In order to break such cycles, it's necessary to bring our wants to the conscious level. They are always down in the unconscious, running our lives, propelling us into unproductive cycles of behavior, until, lov-ingly, we bring them to the surface to have a look at them. It is as if our wants keep us straining at an invisible leash. When we bring these wants and needs to the conscious level, then we can relax and see if we want to act on them. Then also we have the freedom to let them go. Many of the Eastern religions teach the importance of giving up wants. Here we are saying that we must first give ourselves permission to want what we want *consciously,* so that we can either put our wants out into the world to work for us or let them go.

In many situations we may want several different things simultaneously. A man on his way to a party may consciously want to have a good time, but because of old programs, he may also want to act like a clown, to flirt with several women, and to start an argument with his wife. Unconsciously, then, he is wanting a number of conflicting things, and he will very likely get them.

We must be careful of our ten-dency to criticize ourselves for the things we want. In the example above, it would be easy to be hard on the person for wanting such destructive things for himself. However, we must remember that we are always doing exactly what we need to do in every situation, and our unconscious is making decisions based on past experiences, messages we have re-ceived, and what we feel to be in the interest of our survival.

In any case, it's liberating to let those unconscious wants become conscious, no matter how silly or destructive they seem, so that we can see them clearly. For example, once a person knows that one of his wants is to act like a clown, he can either give it up, or go about it with clarity and purpose.

These simple steps are in themselves a path to liberation. Within each step is contained the seed of full enlightenment. The first step, observation, has always been a keystone of personal growth. Observation, seeing things the way they are, is often the only thing that needs to be done.

Other steps involve aligning the mind and the body with *what is*, giving ourselves permission to go deeper into our own experience. For many, parental and societal conditioning taught us to see the world in a certain biased way while at the same time it led us away from experiencing things deeply. Every time a prejudice is installed or we are talked out of a feeling ("There's nothing to be afraid of," "Big boys don't cry"), we are led away from ourselves and conditioned to accept someone else's description of the world. To transcend this layer of conditioning, one must watch it and go deeply into the feelings beneath it.

And love, of course, is everything. Not the love that is born of desire, the kind we hear about in popular songs, but the love that grows as the various layers of what is *not us* are dissolved. As we approach the core of ourselves through observation and deep experience, love grows naturally. Real love can almost be defined in terms of the warm and benevolent acceptance of ourselves and others as we dissolve the layers of conditioning that separate us from our core. We are all capable of loving ourselves for being right where we are. Love will expand naturally as we become unified with ourselves, which in turn makes it possible for us to come into union with others and with the universal. The beauty is that all of this love is available every moment. We can find it by going deeper into where we are, loving ourselves for *what is* within us, even when we are stuck deeply in fear, anger, or self-hatred. We have everything we need to go all the way: awareness, which is our human birthright, and a capacity for deep experience and love. By harmonizing ourselves with *what is*, we join the creative flow that is always present; the flow will then bring us into contact with whatever we need to keep growing. If what we need is a relationship, it will happen; if our bodies need tuning, we will introduce into our lives a nutritionist, a yoga teacher, or a good physician. There's lots of help out there, and absolutely no need to do it all alone.

Early in this chapter, we said that there is one thing we are doing wrong to complicate our lives. In a word, our problem is resistance. The solution is experience, deep flowing experience. And love—to top it all off. Try dropping all resistance to yourself. When the brakes are released you may find that the ride smooths out.

In this chapter we have looked at the basic process by which we change and grow. The process works at all levels, for all problems that the authors have yet experienced. In teaching this process, the authors have found that the main blocks seem to be in the body—the physical storehouse for all our unintegrated feelings—and in communication—our attempts to make contact with each other on the verbal level. Since we spend our whole lives living in our bodies, and since so much of our lives is spent in relationship with one another, the next three chapters are devoted to looking more closely at these two areas.

5

CENTERING THE BODY AND MIND

As we go deeply into the process of making ourselves whole, one goal that emerges is to have a well-tuned body, one that is relaxed, healthy, and sensitive to one's feelings and sensations. Since our feelings are highly physical, we need to tune our bodies so we can feel our own feelings and resonate with the feelings of others. Another goal is to develop a clear, calm mind that is creative, flexible, and free of conditioning. Before we look at how we may accomplish these goals, let us see how we let the beautiful instruments that are our bodies and minds get out of tune in the first place.

Storing Unintegrated Feelings in the Body

When we leave behind unintegrated feelings, they are stored in the body to create tension, imbalance, potential for illness, and fuel for mental self-deception. Here's how.

Every feeling has an accompanying physical manifestation. The same is true for thoughts—mental activities are accompanied by corresponding physical activities. When we are scared, for example, we simultaneously tense our shoulders and our stomachs. In addition, studies have been done in which the thought of something scary (for instance, handling a snake) has evoked the same physical responses as actually handling the snake. Palms sweated, hearts beat faster, muscles tensed. This is the scientific verification of the old cliché, "I got scared just thinking about it."

When we allow ourselves to feel our feelings deeply, the body discharges the energy that the emotion has built up inside us. When the feeling is deeply felt and/or expressed, the stress that builds up when there is a feeling present within us is released. When the stress dissolves, the body returns to optimum "tune" and balance.

When we deny our feelings, however, shut them off without expression, or allow ourselves to feel them only partially, we build up the stress but do not allow it to discharge. Unfinished business is left behind, and the stress stays with us until the unfinished business is expressed.

The body's unfinished business can express itself in several ways. Feelings that are not deeply felt and expressed clearly on the conscious level are most often expressed on the unconscious level through excess muscle tension. When there are unintegrated feelings present in the body, our muscles retain an excessive level of tension, as if straining to contain the feelings. Another way unintegrated feeling is manifested is through excess activity of the autonomic nervous system. The heart beats faster, hands are clammy, the breath is short and shallow. A third type of physical manifestation is through illness. Sometimes the body overloads with unintegrated feeling to the degree that the system malfunctions. The malfunction is often located in the place where the feelings are trapped. Thus, a man who "chokes back" anger may contract a strep throat, while a woman with chronic fear of sexual expression may develop a cervical cancer.*

The final type of physcial manifestation we will discuss here is imbalance. When we are in thrall to unintegrated feelings, our bodies are pulled out of alignment. Let us illustrate the problem with a physical example. One of the authors (G.H.) hurt his knee very badly in an accident when he was seventeen. The healing process was slow, and, impatient, he began to walk on it too soon. In order to protect the knee from pain and further injury, the body compensated by shifting its center of gravity off-center. One shoulder was carried higher than the other, and a hip shifted position in the socket. Unconsciously, adjustments were made throughout the body to protect the knee. The same process is at work with emotional pain. Because we do not understand that the only way out of emotional pain is through it, we protect areas of unintegrated feeling by with-

*While these examples are drawn from real cases, it should not be assumed that all cases of strep throat, cervical cancer, or any other illness are of emotional origin.

drawing awareness from them. As in the knee example, the body compensates for the pain by placing tension elsewhere, thereby pulling the body off-center.

Recall some of the steps in dealing with feelings, described in the last chapter.

¤ *observing them*

¤ *letting ourselves feel them deeply*

¤ *loving ourselves for feeling them*

¤ *expressing them clearly and directly to ourselves and others if it is appropriate at the time*

¤ *determining what we want*

When we fail to deal with our feelings in these ways, the feelings become stuck inside—unobserved, unfelt, unloved, and unexpressed. To contain these feelings we bind them in muscle tension. But they *will* seek attention and expression. If we do not attend to them lovingly and express them clearly, they will express themselves through unconscious channels. These channels are uncomfortable tension, imbalance, repetitive thoughts, emotions, and actions. If our feelings severely need attention and expression, they will get our attention through more drastic means such as sickness and accident.

In addition, when we have unintegrated feelings lodged in our bodies, they create blocks that make us blind to those same feelings in others. Blindness in the feeling domain means that we are not as empathic to others' feelings, that we are confused as to the source of others' actions. In essence, then, the wall between us and our feelings becomes a wall also between us and the feelings of others.

Feelings that go unintegrated over long periods of time create long-term patterns of physical tension and imbalance. For example, two things that many people do when they are scared is hunch their shoulders and tense their stomachs. If a person is scared on a long-term basis (as many of us are in childhood and later), and if the person has no tools to deal with the fear, the unintegrated feelings will lodge in the body as chronically tensed shoulders and stomach. Since the body can maintain its structure nearly indefinitely, the pattern of tension will often remain long after the person has left the original scary situation. Thus, we may be attempting to live in the here and now in a body that was warped to fit past situations.

While this situation may sound dire, it is actually quite positive, for we can use our difficulties on the physical level as cues to point us toward a deeper and more loving acceptance of ourselves on more basic levels, such as the feeling level. If we look at our physical tensions, illnesses, and other difficulties simply as clues we can use on a deeper search for ourselves, there emerge a number of things we can do to use the body more effectively as a tool of psychological and spiritual growth.

One thing we can do to tune the body is to practice one or more of the gentle forms of bodywork that have emerged from spiritual disciplines around the world. Hatha yoga, which comes from the Indian spiritual tradition, is an example, as is Tai Chi Chuan, which comes from the Taoist tradition in China. Both of these forms involve slow, gentle movements that stretch the body and release tension from it.

There are also systems of relaxation training that can bring the body to an unusually deep state of quietude. Progressive Relaxation, a system developed in America by physician Edmund Jacobson, is an example of this genre, as is Kum Nye, a set of procedures from the Tibetan Buddhist tradition. Both of these techniques make use of the power of the mind to relax the body.

There are also systems of bodywork that involve direct manipulation of the body by a therapist. One of these techniques, Structural Integration (developed by Dr. Ida Rolf and commonly known as Rolfing) is perhaps the most immediately dramatic in its effects, as it brings about not only emotional release but a complete restructuring of the body as well. It can be very painful, since the Rolfer stretches tense muscles and realigns the body through physical pressure with his or her knuckles and elbows. Bioenergetics and Reichian therapy can also be mentioned in this context, since both of these body therapies involve direct physical contact by a therapist along with exercises and breathing techniques designed to release pent-up emotions.

There are some gentle, painless techniques that may ultimately accomplish the same goals. The Alexander Technique, developed by the late F.M. Alexander, is an exquisitely gentle approach that slowly resculptures the body by teaching the student to eliminate excess tension from ordinary movement. The Rolf-Aston system of Structural Patterning, which grew out of Rolfing, is somewhat similar to the Alexander approach, although it draws upon Rolf's theories of how the fully functioning body should work. The Feldenkrais method and the Mensendieck technique are two other approaches that involve gentle contact along with learning to perform movements effortlessly.

The approaches mentioned thus far are some of the more prominent ones. For those who want a complete compendium of body therapies, excellent books are available.* Each of the approaches has its own enthusiasts, but after trying them all, the authors conclude that no matter what the approach, if it helps the body increase its freedom of movement, reduce tension, and feel its

---

The Body Reveals, by Ron Kurtz and Hector Prestera (New York: Harper & Row, 1977) is well worth attention. Its bibliography should provide further direction.

feelings more deeply, it is a good technique. And if during the learning and the practice of the approach, there is love shared between teacher and student, client and therapist, the experience can be beautiful indeed.

Unintegrated Feelings
in the Mind

Unintegrated feelings manifest themselves in the mind in several ways. One of the primary ways is in the form of un-invited thoughts. Many, if not all of us, experience memories from the past, fantasies of the future, and self-talk, among other mental events, as we go around in the world. In general, these uninvited mental activities do us very little good and may, in fact, be one of the major ingredients in our suffering, since we often take such mental creations seriously. So, one of our goals as we harmonize ourselves is to reduce the number of thoughts that intrude uninvited upon the mind.

Other mental symptoms of un-integrated feelings are belief, opinion, and point of view. The basic idea here is that the mind stitches together beliefs and opinions out of the fabric of thought in order to defend against unfinished emotional business. An example of belief that is born of unintegrated feeling is the statement re-ferred to earlier in the book in which the client said, "Men can't be trusted." The person had an experience that left behind many unintegrated feelings. Since she could not handle this emotional overload, she formed a belief or opinion ("Men can't be trusted") on the mental level to defend against those leftover feelings. When she feels the wave of archaic anger or fear well up in her body, her mind explains away the feeling with the opinion.

There are chiefly two ways to acquire a belief, opinion, or point of view. One way is to have an experience that leaves behind enough unfinished business to provide a breeding ground for the belief. Another way is to acquire the belief outright, with no experience attached, from another source such as parents, church, school, or the media. For example, a child might acquire the belief, "Divorce is wrong," from a church source, without actually being exposed to divorce personally. With or without direct experience, the belief or opinion is worthless, because it is a rigid structure that keeps us from inquiring into the source of the rigidity. In addition, belief and opinion form barriers between us and others, preventing closeness and sharing.

Point of view is perhaps more troublesome than belief and opinion, simply because of its greater subtlety. While belief and opinion, quite elusive themselves, can be grasped and phrased ("I believe that men can't be trusted"), our points of view are very difficult to transcend because they represent the very ways we see the world. Since we see the world in a certain way, we are inclined to think that the world *is* that way. Some people see the world as being full of people who are out to get them. Since that is how they see the world, that is the way their world is. Others may view the world from the point of view that "I'm right and everyone else is wrong." It is easy to see from these points of view the world would seem a very unstable, discordant place.

There are several things that can help the mind slip free of the strait jackets of belief, opinion, and point of view. Obviously, it is fundamental to integrate all of the feelings that support our mental self-deceptions. To aid this process, the simplest and most effortless thing to do is to observe the mind in all its workings, using our inherited gifts of awareness, as we go about our daily lives. Another way is to set aside a certain time on a regular basis to use for contemplation and a quiet space to sit down and inquire into the source of everything we know. A third approach is to learn and practice some particular meditation technique. Transcendental Meditation, perhaps the most widely available meditation technique in the world, is a mental technique that makes use of a *mantra,* an internally-repeated sound. The section to follow gives instructions for other types of meditation techniques.

Activities for Fine-Tuning
the Mind and Body

Now that you know some ways to tune the body and mind, here are some activities that can give you the experience of doing what we have been talking about. These activities have been drawn from East and West; they have the common goal of making you feel good and helping you embrace more of your mind, body, and feelings. It would be best if a friend read them to you; an alternative is to tape them and play them back to yourself later. Directions in italics are for the reader.

Three Ways to Calm and Center Your Body

Letting Go

This process can be used for getting to sleep at night or at any other time when you need to get your muscles completely relaxed. To do it, find a place to lie down where you can feel comfortable and at ease.

"Wiggle around a bit until you get your body just where it feels best. Uncross your legs, let your arms be at your sides, supported completely by the floor. Let your eyes close.

"Now make a fist with your right hand. Hold the tension for a moment, tighter . . . tighter (*hold 5–10 seconds, on the average*) . . . now let go and let the tension drain out of that hand. . . ."

(*Pause 10 seconds.*)

"Feel the difference between tension and relaxation in your

hand. Now tighten your right forearm and biceps. Hold the tension, study it, then relax and let go, letting all the tension drain out."

(Pause 10 seconds.)

"Now you can tense your right shoulder . . . hold the tension . . . tighter . . . now let go and feel the soothing feeling of relaxation go down your arm."

(Pause 10 seconds.)

"Now sense the difference between your right arm and your left arm."

(Pause 5 seconds.)

"Now tense your left hand. Hold it . . . then let go and let the tension drain out."

(Pause 10 seconds.)

"Now tense your left forearm and bicep. Hold it . . . then let go, feeling very relaxed."

(Pause 10 seconds.)

"Now tense your left shoulder. Hold the tension, study it . . . then let go, letting all the tension drain out."

(Pause 10 seconds.)

"Now you can let arms, hands, and shoulders be relaxed, completely supported by the floor, letting go very, very deeply."

(Pause 5 seconds.)

"Now tense your face all over. Make a face, clench your jaw, squint your eyes. Hold the tension . . . then let go, letting your face become very, very relaxed."

(Pause 10 seconds.)

"Now press your tongue to the roof of your mouth. Tense your throat and jaw . . . hold it . . . study the tension . . . then let go completely, relaxing your throat and jaw."

(Pause 10 seconds.)

"Now tense your chest, tighten up around your heart . . . hold it . . . now let go and relax your chest."

(Pause 10 seconds.)

"Now tighten your stomach . . . hold the tension . . . now let go and feel your stomach relax."

(Pause 10 seconds.)

"Now tighten your pelvis and buttocks . . . hold the tension . . . now relax and let go, feeling your pelvis and buttocks relax."

(Pause 10 seconds.)

"Now tighten your calves and feet . . . hold it . . . then let go and relax completely."

(Pause 10 seconds.)

"Now sense your whole body, just listen to it . . . if you find a tense place, tighten it for a moment and let it go. Your whole body relaxes and feels comfortable and supported by the floor. No effort is required . . . you can feel relaxed and peaceful . . . just let go and let the soothing feeling of relaxation cascade down through your body. You can enjoy this state for as long as you want. When you're ready to come back, signal by raising a finger on your right hand."

(Pause and wait for signal.)

"Now as I count down from ten to one you can let your body and mind wake up again. When I reach one you can open your eyes and sit up feeling rested and alert."

(Count 10–9–8–7–6–5–4–3–2–1.)

Breathing Away Tension

Here is a relaxation process that uses the natural, simple act of breathing to help the person slip into a relaxed, calm state. It can best be done lying down with eyes closed.

"Close your eyes and let your body and mind settle down. Put your right hand gently on your stomach, and your left hand on your chest. Now for a moment just get in touch with the rising and falling of your hands."

(Pause 30–60 seconds.)

"Now begin breathing in through your nose and out through your mouth. After you have let all your breath out, pause for a moment and let your breath surprise you when it comes back in."

(Pause 30 seconds.)

"It's important not to hold your breath—simply pause and wait until it starts spontaneously."

(Continue for 5–10 minutes.)

"Now you may let your breath return to normal. And when you feel ready, gently let your eyes open and sit up feeling rested and alert."

Dissolving Tension

We can relax our bodies by getting in touch with the places where we carry tension, then dissolving that tension with the power of the mind. This process may be done either sitting comfortably or lying down.

"Let your body shift around until it finds a good resting place."

(Pause.)

"Now let your eyes close and follow your breath gently in and out of your body."

(Pause 15 seconds.)

"Now picture a knot in the middle of your forehead . . . this knot holds the tension you feel in your head. Be aware of this knot . . . then let it untie . . . all of your tension melts away."

(Pause 10 seconds.)

"Now imagine a knot in your throat . . . this knot represents all the feelings you've choked back, all the needs you've never expressed. Picture the knot . . . now let it untie and melt."

(Pause 10–30 seconds.)

"Now imagine a knot in your chest . . . this knot keeps all of the tension in your chest. Picture it . . . feel it . . . now let it untie and melt."

(Pause 10–30 seconds.)

"Now imagine a knot in your stomach . . . feel it, see it . . . then let it untie."

(Pause 10–30 seconds.)

"Picture a knot in your pelvis . . . this is the knot that holds your tension in your pelvis and buttocks. Feel it . . . then let it untie."

(Pause 10–30 seconds.)

"Now imagine a deep knot between your navel and your spine . . . that knot holds all the tension in your body. Feel it for a moment . . . then let it untie.

"You can enjoy your relaxation for as long as you want. When you feel like coming back, signal with a finger."

(Pause.)

"Now I'll count backwards from ten to one, and when I hit one you can sit up, feeling rested and alert."

(Count 10–9–8–7–6–5–4–3–2–1.)

*Three Ways to Calm
and Center Your Mind*

Basic Zen Meditation
In meditation the mind is allowed to settle down by attending gently to a pleasant sound or, as in this activity, to the

natural process of breathing. People who meditate regularly swear by it. The authors, both longtime meditators, credit meditation with adding one hundred percent extra energy to their lives. As to the feeling one gets from meditation, one person compared his mind before and after meditation to the feeling of his face before and after washing it in the morning. This process is best done sitting comfortably with eyes closed.

"Relax for a moment, then gently begin to attend to your breathing. Pick a place where you can feel the breath coming in and out of your body—perhaps the tip of your nose or your lungs. Just breathe naturally and attend to your health."

(Pause 1–2 minutes.)

"Your mind will wander. That's fine. As soon as you think of it, you can gently return to paying attention to your breathing. This process of going back and forth between thoughts and paying attention is the process of meditation."

(Pause as long as the person wishes; 10–20 minutes is a good period to begin with.)

"When you're ready to stop meditating, just relax for a minute or two or let your thoughts turn to the outside, then open your eyes."

The Insight Meditation

"Sit comfortably, take a deep breath, and let your body go. Let yourself go and be as relaxed as you can let yourself be."

(Pause 5 seconds.)

"Gently let your eyes close . . . just let them relax in the darkness."

(Pause 5 seconds.)

"Be watching your thoughts as they go through your mind. Every time you spot one that's a memory, say to yourself, 'Memory, memory,' and just gently return to watching. Do the same for fantasies and talk. If you find yourself having a fantasy or listening to talk, just say, 'Fantasy, fantasy' or 'Talking, talking,' and go back to watching. Label each thought in this way. If something else happens (like hearing music) label that, too. If you're not sure what it is, just say 'Thinking, thinking.'"

(Continue for 3–4 minutes at first, working up to about 10 minutes.)

Then, for another day:

"Sit comfortably, take a good, deep breath, and let your body and mind relax. Let your system settle down gently."

(Pause 5–10 seconds.)

"Recently we've been exploring our minds by watching our thoughts and gently labeling them. When we see a memory, we say in our minds, 'Memory, memory,' and when we see a fantasy we say, 'Fantasy, fantasy.' When we hear ourselves talking to ourselves, we say, 'Talking, talking.' Now let's add to that a new type of observing and labeling. As you relax and go inside, notice the rising and falling of your breath. Just pay attention to it in a gentle, nonpossessive way, and when you feel your breath come in, say to yourself, 'Rising, rising,' and when your breath goes out, say 'Falling, falling.' When your mind wanders, which it will, see where it goes, make a mental note, such as, 'Talking, talking,' or 'Thinking, thinking,' then return to your breath, 'Rising, rising,' and 'Falling, falling.' Now close your eyes and begin."

(Continue for 5–10 minutes.)

For another day:

"Sit gently and let your body relax."

(Pause 5–10 seconds.)

"Remember how you observed and labeled your breathing and your thoughts by saying to yourself, 'Rising, rising,' 'Falling, falling,' and 'Memory, memory,' 'Fantasy, fantasy,' or 'Talking, talking.' Today we'll do all of that, and also we'll explore some new types of awareness. Sometimes we have feelings inside of us. Sometimes all we notice about them is that they are pleasant or unpleasant. Sometimes we notice that a feeling is some particular emotion, such as anger, fear, sadness, or happiness. During today's exploring, see if you have any feelings in your bodies like the ones I've just mentioned. If you feel a pleasant feeling, say to yourself, 'Pleasant, pleasant.' If you feel an unpleasant feeling, say to yourself, 'Unpleasant, unpleasant.' If you feel scared, say, 'Scared, scared' or 'Fear, fear.' If you feel anger, say, 'Anger, anger.' If sadness comes up, simply make a mental note that says, 'Sadness, sadness.' Label happiness by saying 'Happy, happy.' When you're not feeling anything, continue to follow your breathing, 'Rising, rising' and 'Falling, falling.'"

(Continue for 5–10 minutes.)

For another day:

"Now we've learned how to label thinking, breathing, and feeling. Today you label those, plus something new. When you are seeing, hearing, touching, tasting, or smelling you are using your senses. So, when you find yourself concentrating on one of these senses, label it, 'Sensing, sensing.' If you're aware of one specific sense, such as seeing or hearing, say to yourself, 'Seeing, seeing' or 'Hearing, hearing.' Do the same with the other senses. When you're not aware of any senses, note your breathing, 'Rising, rising,' 'Falling, falling,' and your thoughts and feelings."

(Continue for 5–10 minutes.)

White Light

This process is a quick purifier and energizer that can pick you up when you're tired. It has been used to cure people of various illnesses. It can be done lying down or sitting up.

"Close your eyes and let your body relax. Move around until you find a spot that's comfortable."

(Pause 10 seconds.)

"Now picture a pure, soothing white light coming into your feet . . . you can relax your feet and let the white light move up to your ankles."

(Pause 5–10 seconds.)

"Now let your calves glow in the white light . . . then your knees . . . now your thighs . . . now the white light enters your pelvis and buttocks . . . now the white light enters your stomach . . . and your heart . . . and your throat . . . now go down to the base of your spine . . . the white light comes up, lighting up each vertebra like a light bulb . . . up into the back of the neck and into your mind . . . now all of you glows with white light . . . and now you can bathe any-one you wish to send good will to in your white light. And then just bathe in your own white light."

(Pause.)

"And when you feel like it, come back to the room again, feeling rested and alert."

How to Feel
Your Feelings

Sometimes it's good to get in a quiet space to listen to our feelings. Here is an activity that can tune you into the wide range of feeling in the body. It is best done lying down.

"First, let's relax. Each time you breathe in, tense every muscle in your body. Then hold the breath and the tension, and then release them. Do this four or five times."

(Pause.)

"Then just relax and let your weight be supported by the floor. Give all your weight to the floor and relax."

(Pause.)

"Think of something that you got angry about recently . . . picture the details as much as you can . . . notice where you feel anger in your body. Just listen and see."

(Pause.)

"Now think of several things that you are scared about . . . check to see where you feel scared in your body."

(Pause.)

"Think of several things you feel hurt or sad about . . . notice what you feel in your body when you feel hurt or sad."

(Pause.)

"Now think of several things you're happy about . . . notice what you feel in your body when you feel happy."

(Pause.)

"All your feelings are all right. Feel them, love them, then think about what you want and need. You can be angry, scared, sad, sexually aroused, happy, and excited. Feelings are there to be felt."

How to Love Yourself

Although loving ourselves is the key to everything we do, we learn to put brakes on our ability to love ourselves, sometimes to the extent that we stop entirely. Here is a process by which you can take the brakes off and let your own talent for self-love flow. Begin by lying or sitting down.

"Close your eyes and take a few deep breaths so your body can relax."

(Pause.)

"Place your right hand on your lower abdomen, about four or five inches below your navel. Put your left hand over your navel. Let both hands rest there for a moment."

(Pause.)

"We all have trouble loving ourselves, so the first thing to do is to love yourself for having a hard time loving yourself."

(Pause.)

"And now you can begin loving everything under your right hand. Love it until it feels right to stop, then move your attention up and love everything under your left hand."

(Pause.)

"Now put your right hand halfway between your navel and your heart, and put your left hand over your heart; let them rest there for a moment."

(Pause.)

"Now love everything under your right hand, and when you've loved it just the right amount, move to your left hand."

(Pause.)

"Now put your right hand on your throat and your left hand on your forehead. Love everything under the right hand, then switch to the left."

(Pause.)

"Now you can relax with your hands at your sides and love yourself for just being."

(Pause.)

"And you can remember to love yourself for whatever you're thinking, feeling, or doing. Now love yourself until you're ready to get up, then sit up feeling rested and alert."

6

RELATIONSHIPS: DISSOLVING BARRIERS TO INTIMACY

Our relationships with others —bosses, children, parents, mates, coworkers, friends—take up a major portion of our time and emotional energy every day of our lives. Although our relationships are a potential source of pleasure, satisfaction, and fulfillment, none of us need look to the rising divorce rate or the incidence of runaway children to be aware that relationships can also be frustrating and painful. Often it seems that the higher our hopes for a successful and pleasureable relationship with a particular person, the more difficulty we ultimately experience in maintaining the good feelings that made the relationship attractive in the beginning.

All of us have certain needs that we wish to meet through our interactions with others. The following are some of the important needs that we all have:

1. *The need for acknowledgment of our existence; to be seen as an individual, separate from the*

masses of human beings; to be recognized as ourself.

2. *The need for information; to be advised and shown how; to be given facts and data about how the world works.*

3. *The need to be appreciated; to have our personal qualities valued and sought after; to be accepted and included.*

4. *The need for intellectual stimulation; to be interested, involved, and entertained; to discuss, debate, and solve problems.*

5. *The need to have fun; to engage in playful, pleasurable, or creative activities with others; to relax, joke, and laugh.*

6. *The need for physical contact; to touch and be touched, to be stroked, and to achieve sexual satisfaction.*

7. *The need for nurturing; to receive assistance, support, and understanding; to be taken care of at times when we cannot take care of ourself.*

8. *The need for closeness and intimacy; to share our innermost self with another human being; to be vulnerable and defenseless; to be accepted for who we are without masks or facades.*

All of our relationships, even the most casual, meet one or more of these needs. In this chapter and the next we will focus on the most difficult and most potentially satisfying of relationships—our intimate love relationships. The principles and procedures that we will discuss, however, are applicable to all of our relationships.

The more time and energy we have invested in a relationship, the more of our needs we hope will be met there, and the more disappointed we become if they are not. Satisfaction in relationships is a function of the willingness of both partners to communicate their own thoughts, feelings, and needs in a clear and straightforward manner and to do what is necessary to assist the other in meeting his or her needs.

The Hidden Agenda
in Relationships

Our success in interacting with another in ways that lead to clarity and positive exchanges is often hampered by a lack of understanding of ourselves and our own needs, inappropriate or ineffective communication skills, and the existence of archaic programs in ourselves and in our partners. Everyone brings a bundle of old unintegrated feelings to every new relationship. While, on the surface, our motivation for entering the relationship may be to have fun, share, give and receive love, and provide support and assistance for one another, each partner also has a hidden agenda—hidden even from himself or herself. The purpose of this agenda is to recreate certain aspects of our relationships with parents, siblings, or other important people in our lives in order to experience some feelings from the past that were never fully felt at that time. While our surface motives are valid and real, often the hidden agendas that lie below our level of awareness are more powerful and can create unexpected problems in the relationship.

An extreme example is Mary, who as a child never allowed herself to feel her anger toward her father when he beat her. When Mary grew up she knew that her need was for a man who would treat her with respect and consideration. However, because of her unresolved feelings toward her father, she was also unconsciously looking for someone with whom she could experience the anger she never allowed herself to feel as a child. When she chose a man to marry, he appeared to her to be a thoroughly gentle and kind person. When he beat her up on their first wedding anniversary, she was shocked and astonished. Mary was not aware that her own unresolved anger contributed to the situation that resulted in her being beaten. This is not to say that her need for respect and consideration was any less *real* than her need to experience the old anger. It is just that the anger, because it was unrecognized and unfelt, was a need with more power to affect her life. Until Mary has completely and thoroughly experienced her anger toward her father, this barrier to getting her other needs met will come up again and again in her relationships.

Dealing with the needs and wants of two constantly changing and unique individuals takes clarity, good will, and a willingness to negotiate productively. In order to create an environment in which to have productive interactions, fun, and good feelings, partners in a relationship need to keep current with each other's feelings, problems, and needs. It is a challenging and stimulating task, which can provide excitement and opportunities for growth for both partners. All of us have experienced, however, the frustration and puzzlement that occurs when our problem-solving procedures break down and we feel powerless to resolve a conflict constructively. Generally these feelings of frustration and helplessness or a thought like, "Here we go again," is coupled with the deep-down realization that the problem will probably not be resolved this time either. This is a tip-off that there is an archaic component to the conflict, even if the problem appears on the surface to be a straightforward issue in the here and now.

Joan's husband, Ed, owned his own business and often worked late on an emergency job or cleaning things up at the office. Joan had asked Ed many times to call if he would not be home in time for their six o'clock meal. Ed steadfastly refused to do this, stating that he was the man of the house and could come and go as he pleased. Joan decided to give up her idea that a good wife always has dinner waiting for her husband. Instead, she put his plate in the oven and did not allow his periodic lateness to interfere with her plans for the evening. By changing her response to the situation, she was able to resolve many of her angry feelings toward Ed, which had centered on the inconvenience she experienced when she set aside her plans for the evening to wait for his arrival. At first Joan thought that she had solved the problem. However, she found that she was still upset about Ed's unwillingness to call and grew even more uncomfortable on evenings when he arrived home late. Their fights about the issue ended with long periods of silence between them, and their family as well as their sex life were suffering. In counseling, both Ed and Joan examined the archaic components of the problem. Ed discovered that his resistance to calling Joan and his feelings when Joan confronted him were similar to feelings he had experienced toward his mother as a child and adolescent. He recognized that he was holding on to some old anger toward his mother for invading his privacy by going through his drawers and closets when he was out of the house and for being critical and restrictive with him. He remembered that he had vowed that when he grew up, no one would check up on him or interfere with his freedom. He interpreted Joan's request as an attempt to invade his privacy and reacted with the anger and defiance that he had tried to control as a child. After having a chance to reexperience the old anger toward his mother in a safe and accepting environment, Ed was more willing to listen in a nonjudgmental manner to what Joan had to say.

Joan, in turn, acknowledged that the major source of her discomfort with Ed's lateness were her fantasies of Ed's being involved in an accident. These fantasies had become increasingly vivid over the previous few months. She had also dreamed several times that he had been injured. Joan recalled that when she was six, she and her mother had been involved in a frightening but fortunately relatively minor automobile accident. Joan herself had escaped with only a few bruises, while her mother had been released from the hospital after an overnight stay. Joan recalled dreaming about the accident for several months and then forgetting the incident entirely. She was sure that her fantasies about Ed were related to the feelings of terror and panic she had experienced at age six. Therefore, she was assisted in reexperiencing the terrible fear that she had never allowed herself to feel fully on the day of the accident.

Once both Ed and Joan had integrated some of their early feelings, they were psychologically freer to apply their well-developed problem-solving skills to the situation. As a result of their negotiations, Ed agreed to call if he expected to be late and if he were near a phone. Joan agreed to be understanding of the times when Ed was delayed in the field and unable to reach her. Both Ed and Joan agreed to continue to monitor the archaic programs that had given this problem its high emotional impact. They decided to do some more work on integrating their old feelings and to be more loving of themselves and one another when they noticed the old programs surfacing in their relationship. They agreed, also, to stop blaming each other for the problem and to acknowledge their individual responsibility for making the situation difficult to handle.

When archaic feelings are present, the issue around which the conflict is centered may be as simple as deciding on a movie or choosing which restaurant would be most suitable for entertaining friends on Saturday night. Very often the subject of the conflict is less important than what happens in the process of solving the problem. When either or both parties harbor archaic feelings, the negotiation of a simple difference of opinion can develop into an all-night fight with several days of strain before trust can be reestablished and the relationship again provide the nurturing, support, and intimacy that both partners need. Too many of these kinds of misunderstandings may result in the permanent breakdown of trust and the eventual death of the relationship.

Archaic Feelings as a Barrier
to Solving New Problems

How do our old unresolved feelings get in the way of our solving problems effectively in the here and now? Generally, what happens is that our perceptions of current situations are distorted because something in the situation reminds us of an incident from the past. Even though we may not consciously remember the event, we have an emotional response similar to the one we had back then.

When Jerry shares his feelings with Lois, sometimes his expression is similar to the look on her father's face when he told an eight-year-old Lois that he and her mother were getting a divorce. Although Lois is not consciously aware of this similarity in expression, she wonders why she feels scared and sad sometimes when Jerry is talking to her. These feelings impair Lois's ability to listen accurately, understand correctly, and respond appropriately to what Jerry is saying. Thereupon, Jerry, who has some unresolved anger toward his parents for not understanding and being supportive of him when he was younger, becomes upset. Jerry and Lois quickly become bogged down in a mire of anger, fear, and confusion without knowing how or why it happened. If they could recognize the archaic nature of their feelings and integrate them, they would avoid many unnecessarily painful moments in their relationship.

Archaic feelings can impede our problem-solving process by creating a number of barriers to effective communication. The first of these barriers involves our ability to hear and understand what the other person is saying. When one's energy is tied up in struggling with intense feelings, often one may either not hear accurately what is being said or misunderstand the meaning of the other's words.

Tom and Anne had been arguing for over an hour about whether or not they could afford to take a long-planned vacation to San Francisco. Finally, Tom said, "Anne, I don't think we're ever going to get this straight as long as we're so steamed up about it." Feeling that he had made a reasonable statement, Tom was aghast when Anne said, "You always blame me for everything!" and ran sobbing from the room. Anne, who was deeply immersed in archaic feelings of fear of being rejected and unloved had actually heard Tom's statement as, "Anne, I don't think we're ever going to get this straight as long as you're so steamed up about it." After another forty-five minutes of confusion and frustration, Tom and Anne managed to clarify what had happened and get back to the problem. At this point Anne said, "I don't think we're going to be able to resolve this tonight. Let's drop it and decide what we're going to do some other time." Tom, whose parents had practically never settled a conflict either between themselves or with him, felt a familiar feeling of frustration. He interpreted Anne's statement to mean that she was not interested in solving the problem. He became very angry and accused Anne of being inconsiderate and selfish. Anne, who saw herself as a very warm and nurturing person, was shaken by the intensity of Tom's outburst. However, she was not surprised, since it was only one more piece of evidence to justify her opinion that all men, even Tom, are insensitive and cruel. Anne was the fifth daughter of a man who had been the last surviving son of an old European family. Her father had hoped for many sons. Before Anne was old enough to figure out the reason for it, she had sensed her father's disappointment and disinterest in her. Her feelings of sadness and anger about her father's treatment of her had generalized to all men. Even Tom was not exempt. That night Tom and Anne slept in separate bedrooms.

Both Tom and Anne had difficulty hearing one another because of interference from their archaic programs. In the first instance, Anne's energy was invested in dealing with the conflicts and fears their argument was bringing up for her rather than listening carefully to Tom. In the second, Tom's interpretation of Anne's statement was based not on her meaning but on an archaic program that came out of a number of unintegrated feelings toward his parents.

Just as archaic feelings can get in the way of hearing accurately, they may also impair our ability to perceive and interpret the behavior of others correctly. The next morning when Tom woke up, the world seemed brighter to him, and he decided to serve breakfast to Anne in bed and make up their differences. Finding they were low on coffee, he threw on his clothes and started off to the neighborhood grocery for coffee and rolls. Anne had spent a restless night and felt depressed and anxious about their fight. She was trying to think of a way to make up with Tom when she heard him moving around the house. Still overcome with archaic feelings toward her father, she was reluctant to approach Tom for fear he would not respond to her. Instead she waited hopefully for him to look in on her. When she heard the back door close, she felt a stab of fear and rushed to the window in time to see Tom open the car door. She called out to him, and he waved and drove away. The next half hour was one of the worst in Anne's life. She was sure Tom had left her without even writing a note. She knew it from the way he had shaken his fist at her before he got in the car. It was hard to believe that Tom would behave in that way, but she had seen it with her own eyes.

Since Anne's childhood feelings about her father's rejection of her had never been fully felt and left behind, these feelings could still be activated in times of stress. When this occurred, Anne's expectations of the situation were distorted by her memories and fantasies of her father's behavior toward her. Both what she "saw" Tom do and her interpretation of his motives were far from accurate.

Archaic feelings are a barrier to our perceiving ourselves clearly, just as they interfere with our perceptions of others. When old, unintegrated feelings have been present, we may find ourselves puzzled by feelings and behavior of our own that seem, in reflection, to have been out of proportion to the situation. In retrospect, it sometimes seems as if "something just came over me" or "I wasn't myself at all."

Archaic feelings can interfere with our ability to think clearly about our feelings, wants, and needs, and when there is a problem to confront, we are often hard-pressed to define our perception of the problem in a way that makes sense even to ourselves. Rather than saying something that would sound foolish to ourselves like, "Just because I am!" in response to the question "Why are you upset?" we concentrate on thinking about why our partner's position is wrong or foolish and worrying about the terrible things that will happen if things are not done our way.

When Tom returned from the grocery store with the supplies for breakfast, Anne was so relieved that he had not left her that she was able to put aside her anger and feel good about being close to Tom again. After a pleasant interlude in bed and a delicious breakfast, Tom and Anne decided to reexamine their conflict of the night before to see if some solution could be reached.

It had all started when Tom came into the kitchen where Anne had been repairing her blender and stated, "I just don't think we're going to be able to afford to take that vacation we planned this year."

"Oh, Tom, are you sure? We've been saving all year. We must have enough put away by now," Anne had replied. An hour later they had not settled the question.

Instead of starting over again, Anne and Tom spent a few minutes alone reviewing their thoughts and feelings of the previous night before coming together to solve the problem. Both Anne and Tom discovered that their behavior had been based upon a number of thoughts and feelings that they had not been aware of at the time of the argument. Anne realized that she was feeling scared and angry because she suspected Tom did not want to be alone with her for two weeks. She was sure that the money problem was only an excuse he was using to justify not spending that time with her. Anne also recognized the possibility that her thoughts and feelings might be archaic, since she was aware of her unresolved feelings about her father's rejecting behavior toward her. She realized that the intensity of her emotions the night before were an indication of archaic feelings at work. She decided that the only way to find out if her suspicions were correct or if they were a result of old programs was to check them out with Tom.

Tom, on the other hand, was having more difficulty shaking loose of the archaic components in his side of the conflict. As he reviewed their interactions, he saw that he had overreacted when Anne challenged his statements about the money crisis. He realized that the feelings he had experienced reminded him of feelings he had had in the past. However, he could think of no specific reason for his defensiveness, and he continued to stand firm in his position that there was not enough money to finance their vacation. He was still too close to the situation to see that his inflexible position was a result of old fears about spending money, stemming from childhood experiences when his family had been on welfare.

Anne initiated their joint exploration of the problem by sharing her fears with Tom and asking him to tell her his feelings about spending so much time alone with her. Tom was surprised to learn the basis of Anne's concerns and was able to reassure her that he had been sincerely looking forward to spending time with her and still was, even though they would have to stay home during their vacation. Once she heard that, Anne's head cleared completely, and she was able to identify her wants and needs in the situation. She realized that her first priority was to spend some time with Tom away from the distractions of home, work, and friends. Her second priority was to travel someplace she had not been before. With this in mind, she suggested that they go over their financial status together.

Once she had taken a good look at their bank statement, it was clear to Anne that while they could not afford to fly to San Francisco as they had planned, they would have plenty of funds to enjoy themselves there if they drove. When she pointed this out to Tom, he was amazed. Anne was right, and he had not even thought of that alternative. However, the trip would still cost several hundred dollars, and he could feel his uneasiness at the thought of spending that much money on something as frivolous as a vacation. With Anne's help, Tom was able to identify the source of his uneasiness and see clearly that his discomfort was based in archaic programs.

Tom and Anne had not been able to identify their true feelings, wants, and needs as long as they were intensely involved in their archaic feelings. Each of them truly thought at the time that the problem was whether or not there was enough money for their vacation. Both were sure that their respective positions were right and that the other one was being unreasonable. It was only later, when the feelings had cooled down somewhat that Anne and Tom were able to perceive what their real motivations and concerns had been the night before.

Naturally, when our perceptions of ourselves and others are cloudy, our communication with one another becomes imprecise and ineffective as well. When archaic feelings are present, communication can break down to the point that one hundred percent of what is being said is either irrelevant to the question at hand or inaccurate and irrational, or both. The most practical but also the most difficult thing to do is to discontinue the discussion until both people have had the opportunity to cool off and decide what they want from the situation. The reason that this sensible step is so difficult to take stems from the "hidden agenda" or the archaic motivation underlying the here and now discussion. The person acting out of archaic feelings is not fully aware of what his or her needs, wants, and goals in the situation are, and, therefore, does not have a plan for meeting these needs. He or she has a tendency to feel that as long as the other person is not allowed to win, the situation will not be a total disaster.

When Tom's head cleared momentarily on the night of their argument, he suggested a break to think things through. But Anne, who was already unknowingly frightened that Tom was rejecting her, felt more frightened rather than reassured by his suggestion. Her response, "You always blame me for everything!" was typical of the kind of communication that occurs when archaic feelings are present.

Archaic feelings can also be a barrier to using our creative imaginations to solve problems in ways that truly meet our needs. Usually, when we can see only one or two alternatives for resolving an issue, we can be sure that some feeling is inhibiting our problem-solving ability. In Tom's case, when he realized that unforeseen expenses necessitated using some of the money saved for their vacation to pay current bills, he automatically responded as his family had in times of financial crisis during his youth. At that time, all treats and "frivolities" had been totally discontinued and money was only spent for the barest of necessities. Tom was already uneasy about spending a large amount of money purely for the pleasure it would bring to him and Anne. The unforeseen extra expenses intensified his old fears and caused him to respond in a rigid and inflexible manner. The more Anne challenged his position, the more determined he became that no other solution was possible. His fear caused him to disregard not only Anne's needs and wants but also his own desires to get away and have fun with Anne. Once Tom saw the archaic components of his position, he and Anne were able to think cooperatively and creatively about their alternatives in a realistic way. After several days of thought and discussion they came up with six alternatives for spending their vacation that were so appealing to both of them that they finally settled the matter by pulling one from a hat.

When archaic feelings are not present or have been worked through and integrated, barriers to achieving our goals may be an irritant, but they do not become a catastrophe. We can usually look at the barriers dispassionately, analyze their impact on the situation and decide what the most effective course of action would be without undue stress or emotional investment. Generally, we can identify numerous alternatives and consider each one in terms of its potential impact on the situation. A good exercise is to compare a problem in your relationship that was solved easily with one that created much turmoil before its resolution, noticing the different feelings and thoughts you had about each one. Doing this will give you some clues on how archaic feelings affect your behavior in your relationships and what areas you should look out for.

Because archaic feelings create an imbalance in our personalities that is uncomfortable for us, even though the discomfort may be outside of our awareness, we are constantly looking for ways to reexperience the old feeling and finally meet the old need once and for all. As we have seen, this drive can result in conflict and pain in our closest and most important relationships. The old feelings can fog our perceptions of ourself and our partner to the point that our ability to perceive the current situation as it really is or to communicate clearly what we are really feeling is impaired. At times, the breakdown may be so significant that we are left with intense fears and irrational thoughts and fantasies, making the problems between us seem insoluble. This situation only reinforces the archaic feelings and is detrimental to the relationship and to the mental health and growth processes of both partners. The more we are thwarted in the present in our unconscious attempts to resolve old programs, the more energy we are likely to invest in our attempts to reach a final resolution. Since we are not likely to be aware of the archaic basis of the problem, redoubling our efforts to get old needs met in the here and now generally results in even more spectacular failure. The result of this vicious circle can be that we invest a disproportionate amount of energy in the negative aspects of our relationships and allow ourselves less and less opportunity to experience the positive parts that brought us together in the first place. As our relationship steadily deteriorates from the increasing stress we have placed on it, each partner finds more and more justification for believing the other to be inadequate, unloving, or seriously flawed in some way. The breakdown of the relationship, which will inevitably follow if the process is allowed to continue, will be a result primarily of differences that have grown out of the imaginations of both partners.

While it would be absurd to maintain that all problem relationships can be or should be saved, the fact is that many unsatisfying relationships will improve if partners can separate the archaic components from real differences that exist in the present. They will find that not only can problems be solved more readily, more constructively, and with less pain, but also real differences in needs, wants, values, and goals can be more easily identified and dealt with. Decisions about the direction of the relationship and how the partners can best relate will be made more easily and with more confidence. The sharing that can lead to intimacy will become clearer and more complete. Energy formerly invested in struggling ineffectually with archaic issues will become available for constructive activities and for sharing fun and pleasure with one another.

7

COMMUNICATING FOR UNDERSTANDING AND INTIMACY

With time and the desire to do so, we can transform the problems in our relationships into enriching growth experiences. All that is needed is information on how the change can be accomplished and a willingness to expend energy in identifying and breaking old habits in order to substitute new ways of thinking, behaving, and communicating. It may be difficult, but it is possible. It requires time, patience with ourselves and each other, and the willingness to confront and work through parts of ourselves that we have been unable or unwilling to deal with in the past.

The basic change that we need to make is one of attitude. It involves understanding how each problem that occurs between us can actually be considered an opportunity for both individuals to learn more about themselves and to become more complete in the present by leaving behind the bit of the past that is contributing to the difficulty of the situation. The more difficult the problem, the greater the learning that can take place if we open ourselves to what is happening. It is necessary to acknowledge that throughout our lives we are in a continuing process of growth. While it might be satisfying to feel that we "have it all together," *all of us,* no matter what our successes or failures or position in society, have in common the fact that we have much to learn about ourselves and much to grow beyond. A problem is a gift that gives us direction and provides us with information about the aspects of ourselves that need attention and thought. If we can stop rejecting our problems and wishing things were different for us and, instead, accept them as puzzles or riddles we have created to assist us in learning to live our lives more fully and creatively, we will have taken a major step in changing our frustration, despair, and fear to the excitement that accompanies learning and growth.

Problem Solving
for Growth

The following step-by-step process can be employed to achieve the maximum growth from each relationship problem and at the same time resolve the issue between the two partners without putting undue stress on the relationship. By using this process, partners can work through their archaic programs and maintain the straightforward and clear communication that is essential to the stability of a relationship in which one or both people are changing.

Step 1. Notice when a discussion is getting out of hand. By checking your own physical sensations and thoughts as well as the verbal and nonverbal cues coming from your partner, it is often possible to identify a conversation that is potentially heated before overt disagreement occurs. Review the cues for identifying feelings and for picking up on the presence of archaic programs given earlier in the book. With some practice in observing yourself and your partner, it will become easier to spot a potential argument before it has reached the point of being hurtful or destructive.

Sue arrived home from work one evening to find Bill waiting for her. She was happy to see him and anticipated a long quiet evening in front of the fire. As they were preparing dinner, Bill mentioned that he had received a call from friends inviting them to an impromptu party later that night. Bill said he would like to go. Sue had heard about the party earlier that day and was aware that a former girlfriend of Bill's would be there. Even though Bill had assured her that his romantic involvement with this woman had ended some time ago, Sue felt uneasy in the woman's company. This was a sore spot with Bill who felt that she was being overly sensitive about an issue that no longer had any meaning in his life.

When Bill asked Sue if she wanted to go to the party, she said that she really wanted to spend a quiet evening at home. Bill suggested as an alternative that he go to the party alone. As she responded to this suggestion by saying that she preferred that he did not go either, Sue noticed a tightening in her stomach and a tense expression around Bill's mouth that told her that they might be headed for trouble.

Step 2. Take time out from the discussion. As soon as you notice that there is a chance that unintegrated feelings or archaic programs are a factor in the discussion, stop the interaction with a clear statement of what you think is happening, what you plan to do about it, and what you want from your partner. The earlier in the discussion this step be taken, the better. However, it can still be taken constructively even if a fight has developed.

As soon as Sue noticed her physical sensations and Bill's nonverbal cues, she said, "I'm beginning to feel upset, and I see by your expression that you may be too. Rather than get into a fight, I'd like to take a half hour to think about what's going on with me and then get together with you to work something out. I'm going for a walk. Will you finish dinner while I'm gone and also think about any feelings you might be having so we can talk about it when I get back?"

Bill agreed, but expressed his concern that they would take so long to solve the problem that it would be too late for the party. Since Sue had no idea how long it would take to reach a conclusion but did not want to spend the evening arguing, she said, "I hope that it doesn't take long to settle this. I am willing to do all I can to see that we resolve it quickly." Bill was satisfied with this, and Sue left for her walk.

When taking a timeout, put yourself in an environment that you find helps you to think clearly. For Sue this involved taking a walk alone, for others it may be relaxing in a favorite chair or engaging in some activity that occupies the hands while leaving the mind free to think.

Step 3. Take complete responsibility for the problem and your own thoughts and feelings about it. This is a difficult step, but crucial to the problem-solving process. It is much easier to see the other person's mistakes and inadequacies in any conflict than it is to identify our own responsibility. Taking responsibility does not mean that you must blame yourself or become a martyr to the situation. It simply involves acknowledging that it takes at least two to have a conflict and then looking at the aspects of the conflict that are significant for you. The more energy you spend in identifying the other person's contribution and wishing he or she would change, the less likely it is that you are going to be able to make a constructive contribution to resolving the situation. The more you think about yourself and your own feelings, the greater the chance that you will be able to get your wants and needs met.

For Sue, taking responsibility

meant realizing that this was a situation from which she could learn something about herself, Bill, and their developing relationship. She acknowledged that her uneasy feelings were her own and that Bill did not set out to make her feel bad by suggesting that they go to the party. With this in mind, she was ready to go on to the next step.

Step 4. Identify the thoughts and feelings arising from the situation. This step gives you the information you need to discover any archaic programs that may have been called forth. To do this, go over the problem, noticing any physical sensations you experience and any thoughts that may come up. Allow yourself to fantasize about what will happen and how you would feel if things do not go your way. Name the feelings you experience and identify a reason for them.

Sue's review of the problem resulted in her noticing a sense of heaviness in her body, which she identified as disappointment about not spending the evening alone with Bill. Next, she was again aware of the tightening in her stomach that she had experienced earlier as a cue that it was time to take a break. She let herself feel the tightness, noticing her thoughts and fantasies as the feeling intensified. In her fantasy, she saw herself sitting alone at the party while Bill was talking and laughing with his old girlfriend. As the fantasy developed, Sue felt her fists clenching and identified the feeling as anger. She then said to herself, "I feel angry because I think Bill will pay attention to his old girlfriend at the party and not to me."

Step 5. Identify any archaic programs that may be contributing to your feelings. To identify archaic components, simply ask yourself whether or not these feelings remind you of feelings that you have had in the past. Get in touch with situations that seem similar to this one in some way. You may be able to come up with one or many instances that remind you of this one. Trace the feeling back as far as you can and allow yourself to be aware of how much your earlier experiences are adding to your feelings in the present.

Once Sue had identified her anger and come up with the reason for it, she was able to see how similar her fantasy about Bill was to her actual experience with her former husband. As she opened herself up more to feeling the anger, she also recalled several occasions during her adolescence and childhood when she had felt left out and ignored at parties. Finally, she experienced a brief image of her parents bringing home her new baby sister from the hospital. As the images unfolded, Sue became aware of some fear mixed in with her anger and was able to acknowledge that she was afraid she would not be able to get the attention she wanted from people close to her and that she felt angry about her ex-husband and her parents not meeting her needs for attention.

Step 6. Integrate the feelings. Following the procedure outlined in chapter 4, integrate the feelings you are experiencing, one at a time. Be sure to remember to love yourself for having the feeling, or if that is not possible at the time, love yourself for hating the feeling. Even if you have not been able to identify the archaic program, now is the time to integrate any feelings you are experiencing. It may be that there is no archaic program involved or that the archaic components will become clear to you in time.

Sue decided to return home to integrate her feelings. After letting Bill know what she was intending to do, she went to her room, lay down on her bed, and allowed her fear to wash over her until she experienced the sensation of fear throughout her whole body. Next, she allowed herself to have her angry feelings while pounding her bed with her fists and making angry noises that came from deep inside of her. Finally, she let herself experience a feeling of love and caring for herself and told herself that it was all right to have her feelings and to let go of them.

Step 7. Think about how to solve the here and now problem. Once you become aware of the archaic issues that have contributed to the problem and once you have integrated your feelings, you will be able to look at the situation confronting you from a fresh, reality-based perspective. This is the time to use your problem-solving skills to identify the facts of the situation and develop a number of alternatives for handling the problem. Then you will be ready to get together with your partner to negotiate a solution in which both of you get the most of what you want and the least of what you do not want from the situation.

In thinking about alternatives it is a good exercise to come up with *at least* ten possible solutions no matter how extreme they seem or how contrary to what you want. Doing this forces you to become creative and imaginative in your problem solving and often results in an acceptable solution to a seemingly unsolvable problem.

When Sue began to define her problem, she realized that she had more than one concern about the situation. Therefore, she came up with the following:

1. *Bill wants to go to the party, and I want to spend the evening alone with him.*

2. *I am afraid that Bill is not as serious about me as I am about him.*

3. *I have some old fear about not getting the attention I want that interferes with my ability to get my needs met in the present.*

By defining her problem this way, Sue was able to separate her old feelings from the current difficulty as well as to clarify for herself why she sometimes felt uneasy and insecure in her relationship with Bill.

Next, she considered the alternatives to the first problem she had defined:

1. *I could go to the party and feel scared.*

2. *Bill and I could both stay home.*

3. *I could stay home and feel lonely.*

4. *I could stay home and invite a friend over.*

5. *Bill and I could go out somewhere else.*

6. *Bill and I could go to the party for awhile and then come home for the rest of the evening.*

7. *I could go to the party and ask Bill to pay attention to me instead of his old girlfriend.*

8. *I could call up an old boyfriend and go out with him.*

9. *I could break off my relationship with Bill if he insists on going to the party.*

10. *I could go to the party and make Bill uncomfortable by flirting with every man there.*

11. *I could go to the party and ask for attention from Bill or other people if I feel left out.*

Sue felt that a number of her alternatives were absurd, but thinking of them had helped her to put the situation in perspective. She made several decisions. First, that what she wanted to do was to spend the evening with Bill, and that while she preferred to stay home by the fire, she would be willing to go to the party for awhile if Bill really wanted

to do that. She also decided to share her feelings of insecurity about getting the attention she wanted from him and
ask for his help. She recognized that, if her priority had been
to spend a quiet evening at home, even though it would be
nice to share that time with Bill, she could be comfortable if
he decided to go to the party anyway.

Step 8. Negotiate a solution. Negotiation is a skill that can
be learned. Before beginning negotiation, it is important that
both people are clear about what they want and where they
are willing to trade or compromise. Honest negotiation between two people committed to a relationship has as its goal
maximizing the benefits to both and minimizing the necessity
for either to give up a significant amount of what he or she
wants. Negotiation is not a manipulative game played to gain
power or to acquire benefits at the expense of the other.
Cooperative negotiation often results in creative solutions to
problems in which both people get more than they expected
or hoped for. While it is sometimes necessary to compromise
or to put off the satisfaction of a need or desire, more often
than not it is possible to solve a problem in a way that enhances rather than diminishes the good feelings of both
partners and, therefore, strengthens the relationship. The
process of negotiation itself can lead to increased intimacy
and the positive feelings that come from working cooperatively with another human being.

There are many excellent
books on the market as well as workshops and seminars available to assist people in improving their interpersonal com-

munications and in developing negotiation skills. Each couple needs to find the process that works best for them. There is not space here to review in depth the many excellent techniques that have been developed in recent years, but here are some guidelines that have worked for the authors and their clients and friends.

How to
Begin Negotiation

Getting started is the hardest part. Many times small concerns in a relationship are not resolved because neither partner feels comfortable bringing them up. The result is little irritations that build up until a major confrontation clears the air. Once you know how, it is easy to clear up the small things before they become big concerns.

You will find that your partner is more willing to listen to your concerns if you begin the discussion with a statement that includes both a definition of the problem and what you perceive your own contribution to the difficulty to be. Next, state clearly what you intend to do in the situation and what you want from your partner. Ask your partner if he or she is willing to cooperate with you in this. If your partner agrees, you have a contract to solve the problem cooperatively and can proceed to examine the available alternatives. You may then either reach a decision or decide what needs to be done before a decision can be made. Sometimes an issue may be so complex that immediate resolution is not possible. One or another alternative may need to be tested or more information obtained before a clear decision can be reached. In such a case, setting a specific time to reopen the discussion is helpful. Sue opened the discussion with Bill by saying, "It seems to me that the problem we have here is that you want to go to the party and I want to spend the evening alone with you. I can see that I was not clear with you about what I wanted to do this evening. In the future, I will do my best to let you know what I want so you won't be in the dark about that.

"I also discovered that I have some scared feelings about not getting the attention I want from you. These feelings go back to my marriage and some things that happened when I was little. When you suggested going to the party, I got into some of those old feelings. I have been just working on integrating them and will continue to do that if they come up again. What I want to do now is to look at our alternatives for tonight and see how you can get what you want and I can get the attention I want from you. Are you willing to do that with me?"

Bill agreed to Sue's plan and also told her that he was pleased that she had shared her scared feelings with him, since it helped him understand her better. He went on to say, "I did some thinking while you were gone, too. I realized that I felt angry when you said you didn't want me to go to the party. It reminded me of when I was a kid and my mother wouldn't let me go out to play. As soon as I saw that, I wasn't mad at you anymore.

"It's not crucial for me to go

to the party tonight, but I would like to spend some time with friends soon. I've been working so hard lately that I'm feeling like a hermit. I probably haven't even been paying as much attention to you as I usually do. It's no wonder you are feeling uneasy."

After Bill and Sue had shared their feelings honestly and clearly, it was not difficult for them to reach a decision about the evening. Bill added a few alternatives to Sue's list, which she had edited to reflect the solutions that she considered to be workable and nonmanipulative. They decided to go to the party and enjoy their friends and then come home early so that they could spend the rest of the evening alone together.

The success of our negotiation with one another and, in fact, of our relationship as a whole depends to a large extent on the style of communication that we use. All of us have developed a number of habits in communication that create real impediments to being understood and getting our needs met. Faulty communication can result in a potentially beautiful relationship going down the drain or up in smoke. Most of our lives we have communicated in ways that have prevented others from really knowing us. We have used words to keep a comfortable distance between ourselves and others. It is difficult at first to reverse the process when we want to be close. Just as the young woman who has defended her virginity until her wedding night must gradually learn to let down her barriers to feeling sexual pleasure, we must, if we wish to have close and intimate relationships, let go of the old habits that prevent us from communicating clearly and accurately with our loved ones. Old habits can be replaced with new, more appropriate ones.

Instead of making assumptions about the thoughts and feelings of the other or the meaning of his or her behavior, check out your hunches and guesses. Most of us expend energy everyday playing a guessing game with our interpersonal relationships. We notice a facial expression, a gesture, or a tone of voice and automatically attribute a reason for what we have observed. We say to ourselves, "He's mad at me," or "She's losing interest in our relationship." Some of us have become, with practice, very good guessers. However, since none of us can really read minds, even very good guessers are often wrong. As we have seen, our unintegrated feelings can lead us to interpret even the clearest of messages to fit expectations based on old programs.

The most effective way to check out guesses and hunches is to ask directly. State the behavior observed or the thought or feeling you are experiencing and ask others to tell you their experience. Simply state, "I noticed you turned away when I came in the room. My guess is that you're mad at me. Is that right?" By checking out your guesses you can avoid the hurt feelings and misunderstandings that could result from either keeping silent or making a comment like, "How come you're mad at me?" Being mad at you could be the farthest thing from the other person's mind at the moment.

Checking out mixed messages

can be a little more difficult. It becomes easier to think of an effective approach if you remember to point out only what you have heard or observed—facts—rather than bringing forth assumptions. Instead of saying, "You don't seem very glad to see me," point out the other person's behavior and ask for a clarification. "You said you were looking forward to spending the day with me, and yet you have been very quiet this afternoon. I'm confused. Will you tell me what is going on with you?"

When Sue and Bill arrived home from the party, Bill noticed that Sue seemed preoccupied and withdrawn. He began to worry that he had done something that upset Sue while they were out. He found himself becoming angry and was nearly ready to burst out with, "What are you mad at me about?" when he checked himself. Instead, he took a deep breath and said, "You seem pretty quiet since we got home. I'm scared that you're upset with me. Will you tell me what's happening?" Sue's concern and sincerity were apparent when she replied, "I'm not mad at you. I'm just trying to think of how to ask you about something that's worrying me."

Bill's communication style had positive results for both of them. He was able to find out that his fears were not based on fact. His openness and concern reassured Sue, who was able to begin to talk about what was really on her mind. If he had expressed his guess as if it were a reality, the results could have been quite different.

Making value judgments, blaming others for causing problems, or what can be called, "making the other person wrong" is another way to create a communication breakdown. The antidote for this communication difficulty is to take responsibility for communicating your own thoughts and feelings without justifying them or judging your partner. Blaming or judgmental statements often begin with the word "you." "You make me so mad," or "If you were a little more considerate of my feelings, none of this would have happened," are two commonly heard examples. Often you will hear yourself making another wrong in your thoughts. "He's so grouchy in the morning." "If she really loved me, she'd (<u>fill in the blank yourself</u>)."

Using critical or value-laden words and making statements that attribute blame cause the other person to stop listening and start defending. Instead, go back to your own experience and communicate that. No one can argue with a factual statement about your own feelings, thoughts, or fantasies. Additionally, a positive statement about what you want is much more helpful to your partner than a list of his or her faults and failings. Beginning your statement with "I" instead of "you" will assist you in learning to overcome a tendency to make the other person wrong. "I feel upset for hours when we have a fight in the morning. I want to find a way to start the day on a happier note. Will you help me figure out what we can do about this problem?" Such a statement opens the door to cooperation rather than sounding the warning buzzer for round one. Being as specific as possible about what you are feeling and what you want will increase the chances for a satisfactory resolution of the problem.

Since Sue had first observed her fear that Bill was not as serious about her as she was about him, she had been reviewing their relationship. She discovered that there were many small things about Bill's behavior and attitude toward her that bothered her. He had broken several appointments with her at the last minute, and he often dropped in without calling or went home early when she had set aside a whole evening for him. Several times recently he had forgotten to call her until very late at night. Sue found herself thinking of Bill as inconsiderate and disrespectful. At the moment that Bill interrupted her thoughts with his concern about her preoccupation, she had been deciding that he was toying with her affections and using her as a convenience.

Brought up short by Bill's obvious concern about her feelings toward him, Sue realized that she was being judgmental about his behavior. Instead of making the critical statement she had been considering, Sue quickly returned to her own experience and said, "Bill, I'm upset about some things that have happened lately. Several times you have broken dates with me or forgotten to call until late. I'm afraid that you're not as serious about our relationship as I am. I've even had fantasies that you are seeing someone else and not telling me. I really want you to be honest with me about your feelings. If you don't feel serious about me, I would rather know than be in the dark. Will you tell me where you are with me?"

By not giving in to her impulse to accuse him of being rude and inconsiderate, Sue was able to avoid making Bill wrong and instead communicated in a way that invited increased honesty in the relationship. Unfortunately, although Bill usually admired Sue's directness, he was disconcerted in this instance and responded by saying, "I don't know why you are upset about that stuff. I thought we straightened this issue out a week ago. You know I have been working hard lately. I really wish you'd be more understanding."

Bill's statement is an example of redefining. We have found redefining to be one of the most subtle and sophisticated impediments to clear communication. It involves picking up on a portion of what has been said and using it to take the conversation off on a sidetrack that the respondent is more comfortable discussing. It is a way to avoid confronting the issue at hand while seeming to respond to it. Redefining muddies the waters while seeming to be an attempt to clarify the problem. It can result in the main point of the discussion being lost within a very short period of time. Consider the following conversation:

John: *Will you be able to get my new shirt washed tomorrow or shall I take it to the laundry?*

Martha: *If you'd fix the washing machine as you promised last week, I'd have all your clothes done by now.*

John: *I can't do everything. I'm overworked as it is. I haven't even been able to play golf for three weeks.*

Martha: *Golf is more important than your own children. When was the last time we took the kids to the beach or on a picnic?*

John may never find out if Martha will wash his shirt tomorrow.

In Bill's case, although everything he said to Sue was true from his perspective, his response was inappropriate and irrelevant to the main message that Sue was sending. To avoid redefining, it is necessary to listen carefully to what your partner is saying. If you are not sure that you have heard the message accurately, check out your understanding by repeating back what you have heard in your own words. Bill might have said, "I think what you are trying to tell me is that you are still angry about my breaking our date last week. Is that right?" Sue, then, would have had the opportunity to clarify for Bill what she really wanted to know from him.

Once you are sure that you are clear about what your partner is saying, limit your reply to comments that are pertinent to the topic under discussion.

Sometimes it may be difficult to understand why a particular issue is important or meaningful to your partner. If we make guesses about this, often we are wrong. Each one of us sees the world from a unique perspective. Our "point of view" is a function of our experiences, training, physiology, and our old programs. We waste energy if we try to force others to give up their points of view and accept our own. Although people can and do learn new ways of seeing their world, it is not because others have forced them to do so.

Redefining can be an attempt to get others to accept your point of view. Often you may be unaware that you are redefining simply because your own point of view seems reasonable and accurate to you. Although understandable, this is an impediment to communication. With practice you can learn to substitute responses that clarify or that convey understanding for a tendency to interpret messages from others to fit your own perspective.

Sue's question about his feelings toward her surprised Bill because he did not define his seriousness about the relationship in terms of keeping appointments or calling early in the evening. Without being aware of doing so, he redefined Sue's message to fit his own point of view. It took Bill and Sue some time to get back to the original point of the discussion. Finally, Sue said, "Bill, I don't want to argue with you about last week. What I want is to know where I stand with you. How serious are you about our relationship?"

This time Bill responded without redefining. "I am very serious about you, Sue," he said. "I love you very much. I am hoping that as we get to know each other better, we'll find that we want to spend the rest of our lives together. I think that it is too soon to know for sure right now about that. There are many things we don't know about each other yet. I want to find out more about you and tell you more about myself. I thought you knew that, so I was surprised by your question."

Bill and Sue were able then to clarify their different points of view regarding the keeping of appointments. Once Sue realized that Bill's perspective on that issue was different from hers, she was able to set aside her point of view that broken appointments indicate a lack of love. She found later that she still did not like it when Bill had to break a date with her. She was able to see the problem from a fresh perspective, however, and eventually she and Bill found a solution that pleased both of them.

Another common, yet often unobserved, impediment to clear communication is a tendency many of us have to ask a question in situations where a statement of our own thoughts and feelings would be more clear and helpful to our partner and more likely to result in a positive outcome for ourselves. Let's look at a few examples.

"What do you want for dinner tonight?" is a vague and uninformative question that gives the listener no information about the alternatives.

"Do you want fish for dinner tonight?" leaves the listener with the impression that it may be fish or nothing. He or she must guess about the alternatives and has good reason to wonder why the question is being asked in the first place.

"Do you want fish or spaghetti tonight?" is somewhat better, but still leaves the listener in a quandary as to what the right answer is. This question puts the responsibility for the resolution of the situation on the shoulders of the listener, who has only sketchy information about what the problem might be.

The questioner is most likely to get the help needed, if he or she will restate the question in such a way as to give more information about the problem:

"I am having a hard time deciding what to fix for dinner tonight. I have fish and the ingredients for spaghetti. Either of them would be okay with me and I want to make something that you'll enjoy. It would help me if you could tell me whether or not you have a preference for one or the other of those dishes." Now that the listener knows the full extent of the situation and what is being asked of him or her, it will be much easier to respond. The response will also be more helpful to the questioner because it will be more appropriate to the problem.

Making a statement instead of asking a question eliminates guessing games and eases the tension that can be created through misunderstanding of one another's needs and intentions. "Do you want to go to a movie tonight?" could mean, "I want to go out with you," or, "There is a movie that I want to see, and I want you to go with me," or, "I want to spend some time alone tonight, so I wish that you would go to a movie," or, "I want to spend some time with you tonight, but I don't want to go to the movies," or, "I think you want to go to the movies tonight, and I want to go with you if you do."

Instead of asking questions, clearly state your own thoughts, feelings, wants, and needs. When you have a valid need for information tell your partner why you are seeking the information. Overcoming the habit of asking questions that hide a statement takes some thought and energy at first, but will help you be more clear about your motives and intentions both with yourself and with others.

Just as the way to psychological and spiritual growth is through the removal of barriers to growth, so it is with relationships. "Try to be happy." Many of us have heard this well-meant advice at some point in our lives. We know how impossible it is to experience happiness through trying. In order to feel happy we must remove the source of our unhappiness. Once that is achieved then there is a space for our happiness to flow through. In relationships, just as in all aspects of our lives, we achieve the positive by eliminating the negative. If there is anger between us, then that anger must be integrated before we can feel loving. If there is fear in being vulnerable, the fear must be felt and loved before intimacy is possible. Becoming close to another person is a process that lasts a lifetime. If the process is one in which both partners are learning to love and respect themselves and one another, the by-products will be a lifetime of sharing, support, and intimacy.

8

ABOUT SEX

Sex is all around us. Daily we see and hear a varied array of sexual stimuli ranging from the subtle to the blatant. Cars, liquor, and toothpaste are all sold with sex. The advertising industry leads us to believe that no matter what the weather, the beautiful people frolic in a perpetual sexual springtime. Winter or summer, fall or spring, we just have to get it up and get it on, lest we are found to be sexually inadequate.

Lately, too, there have been dozens of books published about sex, from the lavishly-illustrated and entertaining *Joy of Sex* by Alex Comfort to the many dull and dry handbooks that are designed for clinicians to use with clients with sexual dysfunctions. The point of view frequently advanced in these books is that good sex is a matter of getting all the parts working in the right rhythm and order. Many of us, of course, feel that sex is not just a mechanical activity but something that can accompany love and make it transcendent. It can help us let go; it can make a relationship whole. But whether we see sex as a basic need, a transcendent experience, a mechanical activity, or something else, we all have feelings and beliefs about sex that are keeping us from living out our full potential in the sexual realm.

Most of us know in our hearts that our sexuality encompasses more than friction between two bodies. When sex is right, it's very right. When it's not, it can become one of the most troublesome aspects of life. The chief problem is that sex does not seem to respond to any of our efforts to control it. Sexual feelings pop up at the most unlikely and inappropriate times, and yet when the stage is set and all conditions are favorable, our sexiness may desert us and leave us feeling neuter.

Our ability to feel sexy and to perform sexually is one area of our lives that provides immediate feedback on the state of our emotional well-being in the here and now. A body filled with stored tension and stress cannot respond with the fullness and spontaneity required for a highly positive sexual experience. A mind filled with worries, angers, and fears wanders from the moment, and the sexual experience diminishes in intensity or stops. Two people who harbor resentments or are ambivalent in their feelings toward one another find it difficult to fit their responses to each other's rhythms.

The opposite is also true. Positive sexual experiences can temporarily release the accumulated tensions of a stressful day. Worries may be erased from the mind for the moment. The whole being, physical, emotional, and spiritual, can gain support and sustenance from a tender caress or the meeting of two bodies in orgastic release. Outside problems may assume a more realistic proportion after a highly positive sexual encounter. Psychological theories that relate sexual dysfunction only to an unresolved attraction to the parent of the opposite sex or only to ineffective habits within the sexual encounter give us incomplete answers. Temporary or chronic difficulties with our sexual expression and functioning can provide us with important clues to aid us in achieving harmony with our inner selves. The stresses and unintegrated feelings of the day can cause a temporary disturbance in our ability to perform with maximum freedom. Lack of information about our own needs and those of our partner can create difficulties between us. Unresolved problems between partners or questions about the appropriateness of sexual intimacy within the relationship may result in temporary or long-standing dysfunction. Doubts about our own masculinity or femininity, including unhappiness with our body image or our ability to fulfill our sex role, exaggerate daily fluctuations in sexual responsiveness and can lead to the reinforcement of those same doubts. Archaic beliefs about sex can support long-standing disturbances, which, in turn, can lead to myriad problems ranging from insatiable sexual feelings to frigidity, chronic impotence, and premature ejaculation. Sometimes we experience severe problems with one partner and none with another.

For many of us, sex is a positive experience most of the time. When it is not, we can be philosophical and wait for another day. Occasionally it may occur to us to wonder whether we have the capacity to experience more sexually than we do right now. Often we can enhance our experience and grow as sexual people even if we do not have particular concerns or worries. Through sex we can open to new awarenesses of our spontaneity and creativity. Sex can provide new avenues for closeness and unity with another through transcendence of the self.

Embracing
Our Sexuality

Our sexual response is a unique part of each one of us. It is a reflection and function of our total personality as well as of our relationship with our partner. If we want to resolve concerns and to grow in the sexual area, we should begin with a close review of the total situation. The answer may be as simple as learning a new technique or as seemingly complex as integrating old feelings of fear of being close and of losing our ego in union with another.

Our culture reflects the intensity of our individual concerns with sex. Everywhere we turn we are bombarded with sex information and/or stimulation. Whether we are intrigued or disgusted, we are tied to the problem. We have feelings about the sexual behavior of others only because their actions threaten to bring into our awareness concerns of our own that we would rather not confront just now.

Sexuality, like all feelings, lies outside the area that can truly be controlled by our will. This is not to say that we do not have responsibility for our feelings or that we cannot choose to behave either appropriately or inappropriately sexually. However, we cannot think our way or talk ourselves out of the difficulties we experience with our sexual being. If we try to do so, we will be working against ourselves, and our feelings will find expression in troubling and unexpected ways.

Walter was feeling frustrated and unfulfilled in his relationship with his wife, Claire. Both of them led busy lives, Claire caring for their family of five and Walter struggling to build up his business and provide for the family. Walter and Claire never seemed to get together sexually. When one was ready, the other was too tired to respond with enthusiasm. Sex was OK, but it lacked the spark that Walter remembered from their early years together. Walter found himself responding more and more to the young women who worked for him. He was disturbed by these feelings because he loved Claire deeply and because he was committed to maintaining a business-like atmosphere at the store. The obligatory employees' Christmas party was the setting for an incident that Walter remembered with intense embarrassment. After a few drinks, he had found himself in the arms of his young bookkeeper. Walter had trouble reconciling his image of himself with this experience. "I behaved just like a character in a comic strip. I can't believe I did it," he told the therapist he contacted after the incident.

Walter's life had become too busy to put energy into resolving the difficulties between him and Claire. He had decided that their problems could wait and he could do without sexual satisfaction for the time being. What he learned was that by ignoring his sexual feelings, he had created a situation where they would be brought to his attention more often and in increasingly uncomfortable ways. Eventually he decided that taking the time now to work out his relationship with Claire would save time and trouble in the long run.

What seems like cultural over-concern with sex today is a reflection of the ambivalence we feel toward this powerful aspect of ourselves. On the one hand, sex holds out the promise of intense emotional release and the pleasurable closeness that sustains us through a difficult day. On the other hand, sex brings us face to face with aspects of ourselves that we may wish to ignore. For many of us it is hard to hide from the messages our sexual response is sending us and still get our sexual needs met. In order to have a fully satisfying sexual experience, we need to feel free enough to let go, to give up the control many of us attempt to maintain over ourselves. Letting go can be fearful, because we do not know much about what it is that we are trying so hard to keep under control. Whatever it is, our fantasies tell us, chances are it is pretty overwhelming.

In fact, the fearful things that we attempt to control are simply unknown parts of ourselves. The conflict we feel results when those unknown parts ask for expression and integration. Our total organism is working toward health and wholeness. The parts of us we have learned to ignore and push aside are just those parts that need most to be brought out, examined, and loved. We put them away at one time because we were afraid that others would not love us if we were to express them. Now we can learn to love them ourselves and to express them; thereby using them to enhance our ability to give and receive love.

All of our feelings, including sexual feelings, are positive and good. When sexual feelings arise they are asking to be felt. We can learn to allow ourselves to feel them even though their expression might not be appropriate at that moment. In this way we will enable ourselves to become more comfortable and in touch with our sexuality. Many of us have learned that if we allow ourselves to feel sexy, we will be compelled to act on those feelings. Unfortunately it is not the sexual feelings, but our attempt to push them aside that gets us into trouble. Sexual arousal without the release of orgasm will not result in injury or bad health. At worst we may feel some temporary discomfort, like an itch that cannot be reached for scratching. In fact, as we become more friendly with our sexual selves, we may find the discomfort transformed into pleasurable feelings.

It is almost impossible to live through a day in which we are not confronted with something designed to elicit a sexual response. If the person in the mouthwash ad turns you on, you can give yourself the gift of allowing those feelings to be there. When you are walking down the street, working, or talking with friends and something or someone taps into your sexiness, you can learn to let those feelings rise and subside as they will. There will always be a chance for orgasm later either with your partner or through masturbation if you wish. You may find yourself feeling some fear or anxiety the first few times that you allow yourself this freedom. If you do, just let yourself relax and love your fear as well as your sexual feelings.

Different people respond to different things. Our response depends on our own cycles, the state of our health, and our emotional condition. If something obviously designed to turn you on does not in fact have that effect, don't worry about it. If you think that you should be responding and are not, you can love yourself for being just where you are and for being worried about that. People worry both about feeling too sexy and about not feeling sexy enough. At this point our beliefs and opinions about ourselves as sexual beings are getting in the way of the reality of experience. Everyone has just exactly the kind of sexuality in any given moment that is right for him or her at that time.

Some people worry because they never seem to feel sexy or because they only feel sexy sometimes and want to have more of those feelings. Many people who experience these concerns have not learned to notice their sexual feelings or have learned to call them something else when they do feel them. If you are concerned because you are more interested in a neighbor or your best friend's spouse than in your own husband or wife, you may find that by letting yourself feel and love your feelings about the other, your own mate becomes more appealing. It is not particularly important where or how you turn on. Each of us can learn to experience and love where we are and thereby gently allow ourselves to move toward where we wish to be.

Fortunately, there are many alternatives available today for people who wish to begin exploring and expanding their own sexuality. There are numerous excellent books filled with exercises and ideas for enhancing responsiveness and learning more about your body and how it works. There are sexuality workshops and counselors who work with individuals and couples in resolving sexual dysfunction and expanding sexual horizons. You have the freedom to explore this aspect of your life in the manner and at the pace that feels most comfortable for you. You can remember that your sexuality is unique to you and that you can pick and choose from other people's methods those things that are helpful and broadening. You may feel fearful as you begin to reawaken this lost part of yourself. There is as much to be learned from experiencing and loving your fear as there is from expanding your knowledge about your sexuality.

There is a difference between the experience of not being turned on and that of being turned off. Discomfort or disgust with things in the sexual arena are important clues. Such feelings indicate that there is a learning experience available to us, an opportunity to come closer to who we really are. No one can tell you what lies below a sexual turnoff. Others may have guesses or opinions. You yourself are the one who can uncover the truth by allowing yourself to experience your discomfort and opening up to an awareness of all the thoughts and feelings that emerge.

Learning from
Our Sexual Fantasies

Our fantasies have many things to tell us about ourselves. Fantasies have long been regarded as an indulgence or worse. Actually they are an important tool in regaining a lost part of ourselves. Their message may be straightforward or symbolic. Either way, they can tell us about things that we may be missing, and they can provide a valuable release for those desires that we really do not wish to have met. One of our friends, Lola, was temporarily estranged from her regular partner and had not developed another sexual relationship. Whenever she thought of her lover she was overwhelmed with sadness, and she was not interested in any other men. Lola hesitantly shared with us a powerful fantasy that she had been experiencing in the weeks subsequent to the breakup. She imagined herself having sex amid piles of trash with a strange, faceless man. At first she expressed disgust with herself for this fantasy, but then she broke out laughing. "I just realized what the fantasy is all about," she said. "I haven't thought about Charlie consciously, because I get too sad. But I really miss him in bed. My faceless man is Charlie, because I feel I don't know him anymore, and the trash is me, because I think he discarded me like a piece of trash. I think I'm angry at him, too."

Fantasies may lead us to new awareness of our needs. Imagining being a victim of rape may indicate a desire for more forcefulness from your partner. Imagining making love to many different people may lead to an awareness of a wish for more variety in our sexual experiences. It is then possible that we may be able to get the variety desired from our current partner.

What we learn about our wants from our fantasies and thoughts about sex enhances our ability to meet our sexual needs. Sometimes partners who seldom discuss sex do not realize that they can kindly and straightforwardly ask for those things that they want to experience more. We may also indicate what things are not pleasurable to us and suggest alternatives. The most effective way to get more of what we want sexually is simply to let our partner know what feels good to us. Most partners are very much concerned with pleasing their lover and really appreciate information that helps them to give more pleasure. Sometimes a sensitive person will interpret a request an implied criticism. If this is the case, a less direct approach is often preferable. When you are making love, you can express your enjoyment verbally or nonverbally. Afterward, or the next day, you can let your partner know how good it felt to you when you made love and specifically what you liked best about it. When feedback is given it is most helpful if it is phrased positively and is as specific as possible. Even though many of us feel embarrassed at first, we can learn the words and the ways to express our desires. By loving our awkwardness, what was once difficult soon becomes effortless.

Sexual energy that is flowing freely arises from our genital area and floods the entire body. When we combat our sexuality we find that our thighs, hips, and buttocks are tense and contracted. We may also notice that our breath only reaches the upper part of our lungs and that the stomach does not expand when we inhale. We can increase our ability to contact and make friends with our sexuality by doing some of the exercises described in chapter 5. They will expand breathing and loosen the lower part of the body. It is a long way from the pelvis to the head, but if the body channel is clear, messages can flow freely.

The journey toward sexual freedom within ourselves is full of exciting discoveries. Nowhere else are the lessons of love so immediately and clearly apparent. Our sexual evolution dramatically points up the limitations of the intellect and the will in personal growth. We find that the more we attempt to control the situation mentally, the more it gets away from us. On the other hand, the more we allow ourselves to see our sexuality just as it is and the more friendly, kind, and loving we are toward ourselves, the greater our capacity for expansion and satisfaction will be.

9

HOW TO GET EVERYTHING YOU WANT

Next to our problems in relationships and other personal problems, we spend most of our "worry" time on money and work. It's okay to be concerned about money and work because it takes money to live in a society like ours and because we spend the majority of our waking hours in tasks related to work. However, much worry energy can be expended with little forward progress. Let's see if we can find ways to use the same amount of energy to dissolve work and money problems. Once we have mastered the principles discussed in this chapter to get everything we want in the worlds of work and money, we can carry them over and apply them to every other area of our lives. Here's the guarantee:

All of us have everything we need to do satisfying work, and to make all the money we need. The trouble is, we put barriers in the way of our satisfaction and our money-making ability. The attitudes and activities described in this chapter can be used to eliminate those barriers so that the natural tendency to pursue satisfaction and success is set in motion.

The Guiding Principles

When we examine the factors governing success and satisfaction, we see that they follow the same principles that we have discussed earlier in the book. Plus, there are several rules about money and work that we can learn in ten minutes, thus saving ourselves a lifetime (or two) of experience to find them out.

Waking Up

The first thing we need to do is look at the problems we have with work and money, so we can wake up and see ourselves exactly as we are.

To begin with, many people have not figured out what they want to do. Others are doing something they do not want to do. A third group are doing something they want to do but not making money at it. The first group are confused, the second miserable, the third hungry. All are dissatisfied. In this most abundant of societies, where there are greater numbers of opportunities than ever before in history, how do millions of people come to suffer dissatisfaction with work and money?

Here are some reasons, followed by solutions to this dilemma. One reason is that many of us are stuck with old ideas about work and money that we picked up from parents, teachers, and society. The following are some typical messages that people receive in their early years. All are false, and all have been discarded by the authors' clients, who have then gone on to more successful and satisfying lives.

- ¤ *"Work is supposed to be hard."*
- ¤ *"Money is the root of all evil."*
- ¤ *"Money is supposed to be spent on toys."*
- ¤ *"If you're successful, someone else must suffer."*
- ¤ *"If you're not successful, you're not a man."*
- ¤ *"If you're not a doctor, Dad will be very disappointed."*
- ¤ *"Don't be more successful than Dad."*
- ¤ *"Women must be less successful than men."*

Now, nobody actually sat these people down and told them these things straight out. Messages such as these are often given nonverbally, and in such subtle ways that the naked eye or ear can hardly detect their transmission. Nevertheless, real people have built their lives around them.

If we can take a moment to find out our beliefs and opinions about money and work, we can save ourselves some hard knocks. Here is a test to find out what your programs are about money and work.

Complete this sentence ten or more times:

Money is _____

Money is _____

Money is _____

Money is _____

Money is _____

Money is _____

Money is _____

Money is _____

Money is _____

Money is _____

and then:

Work is _____

Work is _____

Work is _____

Work is _____

Work is _____

Work is _____

Work is _____

Work is _____

Work is _____

Work is _____

Try this sentence five times:

Work should be _____

Work should be _____

Work should be _____

Work should be _____

Work should be _____

and then this one:

Money should be _____

Money should be _____

Money should be _____

Money should be _____

Money should be _____

List three or more things your mother said about money.

1. _____
2. _____
3. _____

List three or more things your mother said about work.

1. _____
2. _____
3. _____

List three or more things your father said about work.

HOW TO GET EVERYTHING YOU WANT

1. _____
2. _____
3. _____

List three or more things your father said about money.

1. _____
2. _____
3. _____

List three things other members of your family said about work.

1. _____
2. _____
3. _____

List three things other members of your family said about money.

1. _____

2. _____

3. _____

What was your family's attitude toward wealthy people?

_____

_____

_____

What was your family's attitude toward work in general?

_____

_____

_____

The attitudes we pick up from parents and other parent figures during our growing-up years are heavy influences upon
our own attitudes toward work and money. Those attitudes
become barriers that we must eliminate if we want to have
our own relationships to work and money instead of the last

generation's relationships. So the first step in liberating ourselves is to wake up to the unconscious attitudes and beliefs we have about work and money.

A second step is to become aware of the *feelings* we have about work and money. As we grow up, we collect feelings that subsequently affect our lives. We know that feelings from the past that have not been acknowledged, experienced, and loved will come back to cloud our present. Many of these feelings are about work and money.

Try this experiment designed to open yourself up to some feelings you have about your job and your financial status.

If you're employed jot down three things you're angry about at work.

I'm angry _____

I'm angry _____

I'm angry _____

If you're not employed, jot down three things you're angry about in regard to work ("I'm angry I can't find a job").

I'm angry _____

I'm angry _____

I'm angry _____

Now, jot down five things you're scared about in regard to work ("I'm scared of losing my job," "I'm scared of confronting my boss," "I'm scared I won't find a job and I won't be able to pay my bills.").

I'm scared _____

I'm scared _____

I'm scared _____

I'm scared _____

I'm scared _____

Now, jot down five things you're angry about in regard to money.

I'm angry _____

I'm angry _____

I'm angry _____

I'm angry _____

I'm angry _____

Jot down five things you're scared about in regard to money.

I'm scared _____

I'm scared _____

I'm scared _____

I'm scared _____

I'm scared _____

The preceding experiment is based on the fact that most of us are sitting on many unacknowledged old feelings that are getting between us and what we want in regard to work and money. To expose these feelings and be aware of them is to clear the slate so we can be the way we want to be rather than the way we used to be. Remember, feelings are recycled until they are accepted, loved, or expressed.

Some of our feelings were collected in our personal experiences; others were picked up from seeing the way parent figures felt. Try another experiment.

What were your father's feelings about work?

He was angry that (when) _____

_____

He was angry that (when) _____

_____

He was scared that (when) _____

_____

He was scared that (when) _____

_____

He was scared that (when) _____

_____

If your mother worked outside of the home, repeat the experiment from her viewpoint.

She was angry that (when) _____

_____

She was angry that (when) _____

_____

She was angry that (when) _____

_____

She was angry that (when) _____

_____

She was angry that (when) _____

_____

One aspect, then, of clearing the slate so we can get out from under the past is to wake up to the beliefs and opinions that are keeping us from seeing work and money the way they really are. A second factor is feelings, the ones from the past and the ones we experience on a daily basis in our present.

A third element of ourselves that needs loving awareness is the matter of our wants and needs in regard to work and money. When there is something we want or need that we're not aware of, it goes into "storage" in an unconscious part of us, only to bubble beneath the surface where it irritates us. The way to still this inner turmoil is to become aware of our wants and needs, experience them, love them, and then let them go or act on them.

Experiment for a few minutes with becoming aware of current wants and needs in regard to work and money.

What material wants do you have in your work? ("I want to make $30,000 a year.")

I want _____

I want _____

I want _____

I want _____

What social wants? ("I want a lot of praise and feedback from my boss.")

I want _____

I want _____

I want _____

I want _____

What wants do you wish you didn't want? ("I want my boss to drop dead.")

I want _____

I want _____

I want _____

I want _____

What wants do you consider unrealistic? ("I want to make a billion dollars this year; I want to be king of the world.")

I want _____

I want _____

I want _____

I want _____

It is important to get in the habit of figuring out what we want and need. If we keep our wants down in the unconscious parts of ourselves, they come out in sneaky ways. However, if we can open up and expose them to fresh air, they will either crystallize so we can act on them, or they will dissolve so that we need not be driven by them.

The Five Rules of Work and Money

Work and money follow some fairly simple rules. Although these rules have taken many people a lifetime to learn, you can learn them in a few minutes. Please observe the reactions of your mind and body as you read them.

Rule 1. Look around for something you *want* to do and *like* to do.

Rule 2. Do it.

Rule 3. Look around for ways to do it better.

Rule 4. Use work as a process of centering. That is, get in the habit of acknowledging your feelings, your wants, and your inner and outer experiences at work.

Rule 5. Money chases people who follow rules 1, 2, 3, and 4, and if they will slow down a little it will catch them.

Let's take a closer look at the rules.

Rule 1

Finding something that you want to do and like to do is one of the most important tasks of living. There's almost a conspiracy against it. Early on in life, parent figures and society conspire to create the kind of children they want. A father may urge his son or daughter to become a physician because he, the father, wanted to be a physician but was thwarted by lack of money. Society may attempt to program young people toward a certain type of occupation because workers are needed in that field. For example, the late 1950s and early 1960s saw a tremendous push in the United States to get scientists and engineers for the space program. For ten years or so it was almost unpatriotic not to be an engineer or scientist. Thousands of young people moved into these careers. Then, of course, policy changed and the space program lost momentum. Thousands who had bought the American dream became unemployed. They were doubly bitter, because they had been pushed into careers they might not otherwise have chosen. They had begun on a weak foundation. Many were not doing what they wanted to do. On top of that, they lost their jobs and their high salaries, which they had used to buy all the gadgets that engineers and scientists like to buy. Thirty-thousand-dollar-a-year aerospace executives became $165-a-week unemployment-check cashers. One of the authors (G.H.) lived in northern California (a high aerospace unemployment area) during the late 1960s and early 1970s when massive layoffs were occurring. A number of his counseling clients were bewildered men in their thirties and forties who were asking themselves for the first time what *they* wanted to do with their lives. The theme that ran through their stories was that there had been things they wanted to do in their teens and college years, but they had put them away in favor of more financially-rewarding jobs in engineering and technology. For one it had been teaching, for another it had been a trade, for another a craft. For those who were able to get in touch with something they wanted to do and put it into action, the results were very rewarding. Others could not get through the layers of conditioning to find themselves, and the bitterness remained.

The solution is simple. Instead of guessing which jobs are going to be available and programming people toward those jobs, we can teach people to figure out their feelings and wants in regard to work, and then let society follow, taken in new directions by creative people who are doing what they want to do. And it all begins with each individual waking up and looking around for what he or she really wants to do.

◻ *What do you really want to do?*

◻ *What do you really like to do?*

Career counseling, which is now widely available, is an excellent aid in figuring out what you want to do.

Rule 2

◻ *Do it, whether or not there's any immediate financial reward in it.*

◻ *Do it, whether or not there's any recognition in it right away.*

◻ *If you already work, do what you want in your spare time.*

◻ *Just do it.*

The authors have seen this process work for so many people that it now seems like one of the great truths. Once we have found something we like to do and want to do, our next step is to find a way to do it. The important thing is to suspend all consideration and just do it.

Several things get in the way of doing it. One is that we think we need to get paid for something before we can do it. This is nonsense. Susan was a dissatisfied employee of a publishing company who really wanted to be a therapist for troubled adolescents. How could she do that? she asked. How could she give up a good job for a totally new career? Don't, we said. She learned the five rules of work and money, then quickly she saw a solution. She began working as a volunteer at a nearby youth treatment center. This led to some graduate training at a university, which in turn led to a fulltime paying job with the treatment center. By doing what she wanted to do at first for free, she ended up getting paid for doing what she wanted to do.

Another issue that comes up for people is whether they will get recognition if they do what they want to do. We are conditioned to think that if we do what we want to and like to do, we will be like hermits sitting over in some unseen dusty corner of the world. This fear is understandable. We are taught early in life that if we do what we want to do we will be ignored, even punished.

Rule 3

One of the things that characterizes successful people is that they are always on the lookout for ways to do what they do a little better. This fact is true regardless of what they do. Successful marriage partners look for ways to enrich their marriage, successful salesmen look for better ways to sell, successful teachers look for better ways to teach. Along the way, these people find ways to freshen and enliven what they are already doing. Often, too, they find that the way they have been doing things is better than the new ways they are seeing. That's fine, because the important thing is the search itself. Simply being in the process of looking for ways to enliven your work and your life is the reward. The things that you find are bonuses, gifts for being in the act of looking. However, the fact is that doing what you want to do supplies its own satisfaction, so that you will never feel deprived. In addition, it is much easier to excel at something you really want to do, and therefore you can generate a good supply of strokes through competence. Hal was an ulcer-suffering $40,000-a-year troubleshooter for a major company, but he really wanted to work with his hands. He began taking courses in TV repair at a nearby trade school. This work, he found, did not suit him, so he took a course on repairing air conditioners and furnaces. He loved it. He began working in the evening in his neighborhood for modest fees. Then, when he felt confident of his abilities, he placed an ad in the local newspaper. Soon he had more work than he could handle in the evenings and weekends. Hal quit his industry job and went into air conditioning full time. There was one year when his income dropped, but soon he found himself making as much as he had when he was working for the corporation. As an additional bonus, his ulcer cleared up.

Rule 4
What do we do until we experience total satisfaction in the realm of work and money? For one thing, we can use work and our experiences with money as tools to help us look at our feelings, our beliefs, and our problems in general in regard to those two areas. In this way, each of us can make our whole life a process of growing self-awareness, leading toward liberation from all barriers that stand between us and getting the money and job we want.

A first task is to begin to look at the beliefs that we impose upon ourselves everyday at work or in our attempts to find satisfying work. These beliefs keep us from experiencing work the way it really is. Here are several examples of beliefs people bring to work:

- *"Work has to be hard."*
- *"I have to do everything perfectly."*
- *"I'm stupid if I have to ask for information."*
- *"It's their fault, anyway."*
- *"It's essential for me to be right."*

◻ *"Everybody at work has to love me."*

◻ *"Everybody at work has to know I'm boss."*

Many of our beliefs about the way we have to be at work are picked up from parents, others from movies, magazines, and coworkers we have had through the years. The task is to observe these beliefs so that we can eliminate the screens of conditioning that are placed between us and the world.

As we look at beliefs about work, we can also begin to see how the feelings we have at work color our experience there. Our problems with feelings begin when we put the brakes on them and try to stop them through resistance. Resistance never works with feelings! All it does is drive them deeper into the unconscious to come back at us when we aren't looking. At work, and everywhere in life, we experience anger, sadness, fear, sexuality, and other feelings *every day*. In fact, if we are attentive, we can notice dozens of little fears, angers, hurts, and moments of sexual arousals throughout the day. That is the way it is. We are feeling beings. In addition, there are big feelings so overriding that they can pervade our work. Jim was an executive in his forties who attended one of the authors' workshops on stress reduction for management personnel. His main problems were with overconsumption of alcohol, cigarettes, and food, a typical reaction to too much stress. During the workshop, he got in touch, for the first time in his career, with more than fifty different things he was scared and angry about in his work situation. Some of these things were:

- ◻ *scared that he wouldn't perform well*
- ◻ *scared that he would lose his job*
- ◻ *angry that others made more money*
- ◻ *scared when he made presentations*
- ◻ *angry at his boss for lying to him on a regular basis*

When feelings are not acknowledged and lovingly examined, they run us. When they run us, *we* don't run us and are therefore out of control. The solution comes through awareness, acceptance, and love.

To use work as a process of centering, we need to become aware of how our feelings are manifesting themselves in our bodies. Many people, for example, report that their stomachs feel tense at work. Others notice tension in the back of the neck, while many people leave work with what is commonly called "tension headache." All of these body symptoms are cues that we can use at work to become aware of feelings that need acknowledgment, acceptance, and perhaps expression. The two most common unacknowledged feelings are fear and anger. We need to observe our bodies very closely, to see when we are experiencing one or another of our basic feelings.

When we turn work into a process of centering, it can never be boring.

Roger, one of the authors' clients, was a very successful businessman who spent much of his time at work bored and miserable. He was given a homework assignment to carry a small pad with him at work to note his feelings, his wants, and his fantasies. It turned his whole work experience into an exciting process of getting clear of the tangled web of unacknowledged inner experience that he had woven around himself. He noted things he was scared about, things he was angry about, his desires, and the fantasies that passed through his mind. Although this might sound like quite a bit of extra work, it is important to note that he was simply paying attention to what was already there. As Roger's awareness deepened, he saw that this stream of previously unacknowledged inner experience was the source of his dissatisfaction at work. It was all the little unconscious fears, angers, wants, and fantasies that kept him on edge. Soon he was filling up many pages per week with his awarenesses. Work became exciting, as he turned it into a process of centering, and satisfying, as he cleared away all the barriers that were keeping him from being really involved with what he was doing.

The same process can work for you whether you are a homemaker, a senator, or a plumber. We know of people from many walks of life who have turned their work into experiences in liberation simply by turning their natural powers of awareness and experience on what they were already feeling.

Another important way to make work a process of centering is to get in the process of completing unfinished business. Here are some examples of unfinished business:

◻ *You are angry at someone and haven't told that person.*

◻ *You have started something and aren't working on it.*

◻ *You want to do something and haven't done it.*

◻ *You need to talk to someone and haven't done it.*

◻ *You want something and don't have it.*

Unfinished business creates dissatisfaction. Completing it feels good. The important thing to remember about completing unfinished business is that you don't have to complete it all at once. All you need to do to feel good is to complete a little chunk of it, which will then give you the energy to complete the next chunk. If one particular chunk looks like a lot of work, pick another one that would be easier. We all have unfinished business in all shapes and sizes: the important thing is to make a list and start out. Here are several main categories to get you started:

◻ *communications I haven't delivered*

◻ *things I want and don't have*

◻ *people I'm mad at and haven't told*

◻ *ideas I haven't acted on*

◻ *things I appreciate about people and haven't told them*

If you complete bits and pieces of unfinished business, it will transform your work experience. P.S. It works well in the rest of your life, too.

A few final reminders—to make work a process of centering, you can:

- *be aware of your feelings—fear, anger, sadness, sex, joy*
- *be aware of your conscious and unconscious wants ("I want to make a million dollars,"/"I want to experience failure.")*
- *be aware of your body—posture, tension, behavior*
- *be aware of your fantasies—memories, future fantasies, sexual fantasies, self-talk*
- *start completing lists of unfinished business*
- *start figuring out what you want*

Feel free to jot down your thoughts and ideas; feel free to share them with a friend. Everytime you pay attention to yourself, you get paid back doubly.

Rule 5

People who follow the Rules 1, 2, 3, and 4 are moving into harmony with themselves and others, and when they do, they come into harmony with the universe, so that the universe will fall all over itself giving them what they want and need. We can imagine that a person is like a big radio receiver. When it's not tuned, all it gets is static. However, when the tuning dial is adjusted so that it locks in on the right channel, suddenly music (which has been there all the time) begins to flow from the receiver. We tune our receivers by taking the brakes off ourselves so that we flow with our inner experiences—our feelings, our wants, our needs. As we join the flow, there are no barriers between us and what we want and need.

We often try to get what we want and need by *doing.* Of course, doing is important, but we must balance this active mode with *being,* which is our receptive mode. We pay attention to *being* when we open up to our feelings, our bodies, our wants. Then our doing can come from a balanced, centered sense of being that can get us what we want at the same time that we are learning to grow.

Wants work like feelings. First you spot one, then you let yourself feel it, then you love it and get centered again. Let's say you want someone to love you. You spot the want bubbling under the surface, you feel it (perhaps it's a tugging around your heart), then you love yourself for wanting it. This way, you take the want out of your unconscious, embrace it, then step free of it. It's very simple and natural, and there are payoffs. One payoff is that when you bring the want to the surface and let it breathe fresh air, it can work for you in the real world. Perhaps a larger payoff is freedom itself. When we are sitting on unconscious wants, we are tied to them and enslaved by them. When we look at them and embrace them we are free.

Money is chasing you if you are in the process of harmonizing yourself through feeling your feelings, loving yourself, figuring out your wants and sharing yourself through caring communication. Now, if you can slow down just a little, perhaps by spending ten minutes a day in quiet contemplation of yourself, it will start to catch up with you.

For you see, when we are out of harmony with ourselves, we experience scarcity and imbalance. When we open up to ourselves and embrace who we truly are, we fall into step with the universe (since we *are* the on-the-spot representatives of the universe.). When we are in harmony with ourselves and the universe, there is no scarcity. We can have everything we need.

10

PARENTS
AND
CHILDREN

"I can remember a hiding place I had as a child. I would go there whenever I had a conflict with one of my parents. I remember telling myself over and over that I'd never treat my children the way my parents treated me." Maria was struggling to hold back her tears as she shared her childhood memories with the others in the effective-parenting seminar. "Now I realize that I am just as hard on my kids as my mother was on me. I don't listen. I don't talk to them the way they deserve to be talked to. Sometimes I look in the mirror and see my mother's face looking back at me. It's frightening."

Maria was describing an experience shared by many parents in the group. Most parents feel guilty from time to time because they see that their performance with their children does not measure up to their image of how they wish to be and what they wish to give as parents. People who are parents often find themselves with a larger responsibility than they anticipated before the birth of the first child. Children require a safe and loving environment in which to grow. Parents have the job of caring for their children's physical and emotional needs, keeping them safe and healthy, helping them learn about the world by giving accurate information and modeling effective behavior, and smoothing the way for them to become fully-functioning adults.

It is a difficult task, one that grows increasingly difficult in a society that is changing as rapidly as ours. Traditional child-rearing practices no longer seem appropriate. New theories of child development and child care are advanced regularly. One year we may try permissiveness and the next year we are stressing discipline and limits. We want our children to be themselves, but we also want them to get along with others. We wonder where the fine line lies between the children's ability to be responsible for themselves and their need for help and direction. We hate to see our children hurt and yet we know that there are some lessons they need to learn through their own experiences. We want to be perfect parents, but we are not sure just what that involves. We feel uncomfortable when we realize that we do not have the answers to every difficulty that confronts our children as they grow. We do not want to damage our children by our parenting, but deep in our hearts we feel sure that there are times when we have failed to listen, when we have been harsh rather than understanding, and when we have not stepped in when we should have done so.

No one can be completely prepared for the things that come up for us as parents. We can learn to diaper and bathe a baby; we can even learn how to talk to children. None of this will really prepare us for the emotional responses, both positive and negative, that we will experience in caring for a child of our own. People who have more than one child quickly learn that their experience with each of their children is different. Parents cannot know in advance everything about the needs of a child because they have not yet met that child. As children grow, their needs change. The child we knew a year ago is now a different person in many important ways. This four-year-old is different from his brother or sister at age four. It is impossible for parents to know all the answers in advance. Parents can, however, learn to love themselves for not being perfect and to learn and grow along with their children.

Growing Up
with Our Children

One rarely understood but important aspect of the parent-child relationship is the opportunity we as parents have to recycle our own developmental stages as our children go through the same stages and confront the issues appropriate at each age. A parent who is aware of this process may often find that the stages where they feel most frustrated and uncomfortable with a child are just the ones for which the parent retains the most archaic feelings. Parents may have unresolved feelings regarding their own toilet training or early peer relationships. They may have experienced a troublesome transition into adolescence or had difficulty developing relationships with the opposite sex in the later teenage years. A rebellious two-year-old may remind a mother of her own unresolved desires to rebel, while a pubescent daughter may create discomfort in a father who has problems with his own sexuality. As our child is confronting new issues, we feel empathy but also fear about our own unresolved issues. Sometimes we are at a loss to help the child because we do not have our usual perspective. We may find ourselves angry and irritated by the child's behavior, to an extent that seems inappropriate to the situation.

At such times the parent has as great an opportunity to grow as does the child. Our feelings are cues to lead us to a deeper experience of ourselves, to become aware of and integrate old feelings that may have been pushed aside as we reached maturity. If we follow through, we will often find ourselves thinking more clearly about our child's problem and becoming a more effective facilitator of his or her growth and development.

Joan came to one of the authors because of difficulties she was experiencing with her seventeen-year-old son, Johnny. She had a long list of complaints about him. He drank; he stayed out late; he was irresponsible about household chores; he was repeatedly fired from the odd jobs he took on after school; he was rude and uncooperative with other family members. Johnny often stated that he was going to leave home at the first opportunity. Joan was very much concerned about his plan as she felt his behavior showed him to be too immature to handle being on his own. She had wanted him to see a therapist, but he refused. Joan herself was at the end of her rope. She could not think of a thing that she could do about the situation. Her nerves were on edge and she was losing weight. Everytime she saw Johnny she was overwhelmed with a surge of anger. Their relationship had deteriorated significantly in the previous six months until they barely spoke to one another except in their shouting matches.

In counseling Joan learned that Johnny's behavior was a reflection of his awareness that he would soon need to leave the family and his ambivalent feelings about doing so. On the one hand he wanted the freedom of adult life. On the other he was uncertain about his ability to handle that freedom. His irresponsible behavior was a result of an unconscious attempt to force onto his family the decision of whether to stay or go.

Although understanding the situation helped Joan, she found herself no better able to handle her relationship with Johnny. At this point, her therapist asked her about her own separation from her parents. Upon telling how her parents had forced her out of the household when she was sixteen, she immediately saw the parallels between her own situation and Johnny's. Joan had vowed never to treat her children as she had been treated, but her unresolved feelings about separation had gotten in the way for her when her eldest approached the age of separation. Instead of facilitating the transition for Johnny by opening up more and more opportunities for him to test himself in the outside world, Joan had suddenly clamped down on his freedoms when Johnny was in his sixteenth year. Naturally he rebelled against these restrictions, and soon he and Joan were locked into an escalating battle of wills.

As Joan worked through her own archaic feelings, she was able to change the home environment for Johnny and eventually to talk over with him what she saw happening between them. Soon Johnny began to attend therapy sessions with Joan, and the two of them worked out a more constructive method for separation. She experienced other gains from integrating her archaic separation programs. She found herself less jealous of her husband and less fearful about his frequent business trips. She became more patient with her youngest child, who was just entering grade school. Her blood pressure, which had been elevated for years, dropped to normal. She was able to forgive her own parents who had died five years earlier.

When parents can identify and integrate archaic feelings brought up by their children's development, they can then become open to learning the skills needed to solve the here and now problem. Parents have many resources to call upon once they have an idea what their children's needs might be. Books on child rearing and child development* help to provide some insight, and there

---

*The authors have enjoyed Thomas Gordon's *Parent Effectiveness Training* (New York: Peter Wyden, Inc., 1970) and Virginia Satir's *Peoplemaking* (Palo Alto, CA.: Science and Behavior Books, 1972).

are effective-parenting classes and parents-anonymous groups in many communities. Schools have counselors and social workers trained to help families learn problem-solving and communication skills. Your community health center, your local psychological association, your children's school nurse, your pediatrician, or your family doctor can recommend an experienced family therapist.

Many of us are reluctant to seek help when we are worried about our children. We tell ourselves that "it's just a phase" and believe that we should be able to handle whatever comes up. Even if our worries are groundless, consultation with a competent professional can ease our concern and help us to see how we might better facilitate our children's growth within the situation that confronts us. Seeking help in problem situations is more often an indication of wisdom than incompetence.

Helping Children
Handle the World

A major task for parents over the years has been to teach traditional social values so that the children will be able to understand the assumptions upon which their society is based and know how to interact appropriately with their world. In times of transition, where today's value becomes tomorrow's neurotic hangup, parents have a great deal of difficulty deciding what teachings are appropriate. Our children must know certain rules now and be able to follow them comfortably in order to stay out of trouble, but we usually want more for them than that. We not only wish for them to stay out of trouble, we wish them to be successful and happy. Since we ourselves do not have any idea of what success and happiness will entail in twenty years, we find ourselves in a difficult dilemma. What can we offer our children now that will assist them in a society that may be radically different when they grow up?

Actually, this problem may be a disguised blessing. While we may not be able to pass along many rules and maxims for behavior that we can be sure will always be appropriate, we can teach a process for living that will enable our children to learn and grow from any situation they may confront. The result can be that we avoid cluttering their minds with opinions and beliefs that will be invalid in new situations and have to be discarded. Many women whose parents once urged them to go into teaching because it was a career that they could always fall back on, today find themselves without a net. So it is with many of the things we might teach our children based on what is true today. Instead we can teach them to confront each life experience as containing the gift of a lesson from which they can learn more about themselves and about the world. The more our children are free to assess all aspects of the lessons their lives bring them, the more likely they will find success and happiness as adults.

As our children grow we can teach them, in stages appropriate to their development, the processes of observation and integration of their feelings. We can help them learn to love themselves, to be aware of their wants and needs, and to learn to solve problems effectively. We can teach and model the process of confronting life's difficulties in such a way as to maximize self-awareness.

For very young children with undeveloped verbal and reasoning capabilities, the parents' task in this process is to allow their children the experience of their own feelings and to develop an environment where it is psychologically safe to feel and to talk about feelings. Instead of teaching our children to control or talk themselves out of their feelings, we can name the feelings and acknowledge the validity of their experience. When a small child falls and skins a knee, for example, instead of saying, "Oh, that's not so bad," which may be an expression of our own wishes that our child not be hurt, we can instead say something that is more congruent with the child's own experience. Saying something like, "That really must hurt!" affirms for the child his own perception of what is happening in his body and assists him in learning about hurts. Children whose feelings are acknowledged are better prepared to deal with the hurt. The child who knows that you understand that his knee is hurting is more likely to be cooperative as you clean the wound and apply antiseptic.

As children grow they can begin learning that there are reasons for their feelings. Small children have many frustrations in their lives because there are many things that they want and cannot have. The child who is frustrated at not being able to catch a bird in the park or has lost her penny on the street can learn to name her feeling, state why she is feeling it, and learn to love herself for having the feeling. The parent can assist in this task by talking with the child about the feelings and accepting them as natural and normal. For example, one of the authors overheard the following conversation between a mother and a preschooler.

Mom: *Why are you crying?*

Child: *That dumb bird won't stay still!*

Mom: *Why do you want the bird to stay still?*

Child: *I want to pet him.*

Mom: *Why?*

Child: *I love him. I want to feel his feathers.*

Mom: *Are you mad at the bird because you can't catch him?*

Child: *Yes. I want him.*

Mom: *I get mad sometimes when I can't get what I want too. Sometimes I get sad too.*

Child: *Me too.*

In this example the mother has focused on the child's feelings, helping her identify them and understand the reasons for them. By confiding that she has the same feelings at times, she has delivered the message that the child's feelings are okay and not something bad or shameful. This kind of situation is often difficult for parents. We want our children to be happy, and we hurt when they hurt. It is a natural temptation to try to make things better for our children when they are upset. The mother in the example could have told her child that the bird was dirty and germy anyway or explained that birds need to be free to fly around and do not want to be petted. The latter explanation might be appropriate later if the child asks why the bird would not allow itself to be caught. The important thing to the child at that moment, however, is that she is feeling upset. Through her mother's understanding and acceptance of her feelings, she learns some basic lessons about herself in relationship to the world she lives in.

Older children can build on this experience of closeness and acceptance of their own feelings to begin solving problems effectively. School-age children can learn to make clear statements of feelings and wants and develop a list of alternatives for getting what they want. Parents can learn to help children develop alternatives and evaluate different problem-solving techniques without giving advice or imposing their own values. Sometimes children will come up with alternatives that are unacceptable to the parent. In such cases the parent can clearly tell the child that the alternative is unacceptable and explain why.

Paula was seven and an only child. She had had little opportunity to develop peer relationships before starting school and was having difficulty handling playground give and take. One day one of her friends, Chris, became upset with her and decided to play a trick on her. Chris called another of their friends, Judy, on the telephone and with Paula listening in asked Judy if she liked Paula. Chris knew Judy was mad at Paula right then and would say no. Paula was very hurt and went home in tears. She felt scared that she was no good and that nobody would be her friend.

Paula's parents overcame their impulse to call the other girls' families and sat down with Paula to get clear on the problem and see what the solution might be. At first Paula could only cry about her upset and fear. Her parents accepted her feelings and affirmed that they loved her and that she could love herself too even while she was feeling rejected. Soon Paula felt better but said that she would never play with Chris and Judy again. Her parents responded that that was okay with them if that was the way she wanted it. However, they asked her to think it over and come up with five other alternatives for solving the problem. Paula was encouraged to think about how she would feel if someone had tricked her as Chris had Judy.

Paula's five alternatives included taking Chris and Judy's school books and throwing them in a puddle. Her parents explained why that alternative was not an acceptable one and what the consequences of such behavior could be. The alternative Paula eventually chose was to call Judy, tell her what had happened, and ask her if she really did not like her and why. She learned that Judy was mad at her for something that had happened a few days previously, but that she still liked Paula. After several days of problem solving and hurt feelings the three girls decided to forget the whole thing and were again inseparable friends.

In Paula's case there were many lessons both for the girls and for Paula's parents. Paula and the other girls learned some important things about interpersonal relationships. Paula learned that she could solve problems, even very difficult ones. Paula's parents learned that they could help her more effectively by accepting her and helping her think through her difficulties than by stepping in to solve the problem for her. They gained new respect for Paula as they watched her work out a hard problem.

With older children, parents can reinforce the lessons learned in problem solving and help children begin to generalize the learning. They can discuss their own problem solving, their feelings, and what they have learned from different situations and ask their children to do the same thing. They can use examples from their daily life or make up situations and discuss how the lessons might apply in different contexts. Parents and children who feel free to share feelings and discuss problems with one another develop close relationships that support the growth of everyone involved.

Raising children to become competent and happy adults in a rapidly changing society requires a certain objectivity and a willingness to allow children to have their own experience. Parents who still have unresolved childhood issues may find it difficult to attain objectivity until the old feelings are understood and integrated. They can, however, begin teaching their children acceptance and love for self as well as appropriate problem-solving techniques. Children's lives will be enriched as they learn effective living processes.

11

BECOMING SINGLE, BEING SINGLE

Not too long ago single-
ness was a brief period between leaving home and getting
married. Many people, particularly women, never had the
opportunity to enjoy the state of being single. Today many
people are experiencing singleness for the first time, after
years of marriage, and many others are voluntarily choosing
a single lifestyle instead of marriage. For those of us who are
suddenly and unexpectedly single because of divorce, separation, or widowhood, or those who are on our own after
having been pushed from the parental nest, the reaction is
very similar. The natural sadness of loss is mixed with fear:
we are not prepared. For those who choose singleness, other
issues come up that must be dealt with in order to turn the
experience into a time of growth.

Being unprepared for single-
ness can cause the inevitable and natural discomfort experienced in any lifestyle transition to be even more intense and

to extend over a longer period of time. For the unprepared, the word "discomfort" may, indeed, seem too mild. "Panic" and "despair" may capture the feelings more precisely. This transition point is made more complex by the necessity of pulling together a new life just at the moment when we may feel most incapable of doing what previously seemed to be the simplest tasks. We have the sense that if we don't get going and *do* something our most catastrophic fears will be realized. At the same time, we are aware that our state of grief and fear impedes clear thinking and saps our energy. The conflict between needing to act and feeling unable to act heightens fear and may result in wasting energy through frantic but undirected activity. Many people who are single, either by choice or by chance, find their lifestyle to be full of paradoxes. We tend to vacillate between seeing our singleness as a blessing and as a curse. A single person can experience the joy of being free to eat any food that he or she wishes at any time of the day or night. Unfortunately this freedom also means that we must shop for and prepare the food alone, or that we must choose a restaurant in which to eat alone. The single person returns home after a long day at work to the peace of a quiet home. There are no demands on the part of others that can add more stress to an already stressful day. There is also no one there to share the joys and sorrows of the day, to bring a refreshing drink, to help think through a difficult problem.

The Dilemma of
Living Life Single

Single people have more freedom to choose how to arrange life and how to spend their time than do people who live with others. There are fewer responsibilities to others, fewer schedules to be reconciled, fewer requirements to be in a certain place at a certain time, fewer chances for plans to be interrupted by the unanticipated needs of another. The same freedom brings new kinds of problems. When one has no particular requirements to meet in the structuring of his or her time, there are many more decisions to be made. When we are completely free to do exactly as we please, we sometimes find we cannot think of a thing that pleases us. If we have ten alternatives for spending the next hour, how can we decide which one we would enjoy most? If we can choose to live and work anywhere, or to stay just where we are, what basis do we have for making a decision? We may find ourselves puzzled and confused about all sorts of decisions, both simple and complex, when we have only our own wants and needs to consider.

As single people, we experience every day our total responsibility for the life we are leading. While all of us, single or part of a larger family, are ultimately responsible for ourselves, singleness brings this experience sharply into focus. The amount of money in the bank and the busyness of our social life reflects no one's efforts but our own. If we become ill, we must seek out the care that we need. No one will provide it automatically. If we want relationships, we are aware that we must build them ourselves. If we want sex, or to spend a quiet evening talking with another, we must actively arrange for that to happen. There is no one else around to anticipate our needs. We have to define what we want and figure out how to get it if we wish to have our needs met at all.

Single people have the time and space to learn to see themselves through their own eyes, without the burdens of the demands and definitions of others. While there is no one to fall back on in difficult times, there is also no one to blame when difficulties arise. This one fact removes a major barrier to seeing things as they are. Single people, therefore, are automatically one step ahead of others who may see their problems as caused by others. No matter how much we dislike what we see in our lives, or how much we may wish that others would change and make things easier for us, as single people we know that we cannot rely on anyone but ourselves to solve the problems confronting us. With this knowledge comes the awareness that in order to change what we do not want in our lives we first need to have an idea of what we do want. Then we can set about removing the barriers to achieving our desires.

Single people are confronted with the joys and difficulties of getting to know themselves by themselves. The impetus for growth and change comes from within. No one else demands that we live up to their expectations of us. No one else will give us definitions of ourselves that do not fit but that we feel we must try to achieve. No one will be disappointed in our failures to measure up to their ideas of how we should be. We can move at our own pace, focus on the issues that we ourselves choose, try on the roles that we wish to explore. The pressure is off.

As the external pressure lessens, our own responsibility to ourselves is increased. We have complete freedom to put aside any aspect of life that we do not wish to explore or that we find too painful to confront. We may, if we choose, focus totally on our work, spending long hours, even on weekends, pursuing a career and success. On the other hand, we may involve ourselves totally in social or interpersonal affairs, working only enough to provide for our financial support, tending our bodies only to the extent necessary to maintain health and energy for our activities. It is, perhaps, easier for a single person to grow out of balance with himself or herself because of the lack of pressure from others. There is nothing intrinsically wrong with placing primary emphasis on one aspect of life over another at any given time. Each of us has priorities from time to time that may demand a certain dedication. We can acknowledge our priorities at the same time we notice whether or not we are purposely setting up our lives to avoid certain issues that confuse us and cause us pain. In assuming responsibility for ourselves, we may decide to focus from time to time on the confusing aspects of life even as we pursue our priorities. In this way, we may maintain contact with all the parts of us and open the door to becoming a harmonious and balanced being.

Making the Transition
to a New Life

The newly divorced, separated, or widowed single person often is confronted with additional difficulties. There is grief at the ending of a relationship that was begun with the intent of creating a lifetime partnership. There is the necessity of learning the living skills—cooking, financial management, the ability to be self-supporting, child care, among others—that the other partner took responsibility for within the relationship. Friends may take sides, and our social life undergoes dramatic changes when we no longer are a part of a couple. Just when we most need the comfort of a warm, loving body in bed with us, just when we feel most lonely and needy, our primary support systems are breaking down and becoming unavailable to us. If we have to work and also care for home and children, the days may seem too short for us to meet all of our responsibilities and also deal effectively with the stresses of the new situation. Just getting through one day at a time becomes a major accomplishment. The old ways of

Realistically there was not much likelihood that Hilda could come up with a large sum of money in the near future. Although her estate was adequate for comfortable living, she could not afford to travel in luxury and still make ends meet for very long. In therapy she continued to feel her fear and anger about her financial situation as well as her feelings about being useless and stagnant. One day she mentioned to her therapist, "You know, I've always loved antiques. I have several good pieces at home and they mean a lot to me. I've studied and read for years and I know a lot about the subject. The other day it occurred to me how much I would enjoy having a small shop. I could travel on buying trips. I'd meet a lot of people, and I like helping people to find things for their home. I've often helped my friends that way.

"The trouble is I don't know anything about business. I'm just learning to balance a checkbook, and I'd have to find a place and stock it. I'd probably need a loan from the bank. I guess its just another crazy idea."

Hilda was encouraged by her therapist to explore the possibilities of setting up such a business. Hilda talked to other dealers, to her lawyer, and to a professor of business management at a nearby university. Her research led her to some conclusions that surprised her. There were several ways that she could begin such a business and learn the skills she needed to make it a success. She found her lawyer and others enthusiastic about the idea. Six months later she had taken a course in small business management, hired a good accountant, and was preparing to leave on her first buying trip.

"I've never felt so alive in my life," she told her therapist. "I'm starting small, selling antiques of the region out of my home. Later, I may get a shop, and if things go as well as I think they will, I'll be buying in Europe in a year or two. I may never have a million dollars, but I don't think I'll end up in a tenement either."

Hilda's experience is not unique. Many single people have built new lives by identifying the inner needs expressed by their loneliness. At first her solutions were not very practical. She learned in time, however, that some solutions could be implemented if she were willing to gain the necessary skills. Eventually she found the solution that resolved her money problem as well as meeting a number of other needs. If she had not been willing to love her loneliness and its attendant feelings of fear and anger and allow herself to experience her needs, she could not have found such a happy solution.

Demands
of Everyday Life

Single people find themselves responsible for the smooth functioning of every area of their lives. They must see that they have clean and appropriate clothing to wear, that the checkbook is balanced, and that they do not spend more than they make. They need to be aware of their nutritional needs and the amount of rest they require for good health. They must be sure that they have adequate transportation and a comfortable place to live. They are responsible for seeing that their work and leisure time is fulfilling and satisfying. For those who depended on others to take care of any or all of these aspects of their lives, the new responsibilities of singleness can bring up many unexpected feelings.

As single people, we may feel at once excited, scared, angry, and sad each time we realize that there is still another responsibility we had not foreseen and another skill we have never learned. Sometimes we find that new responsibilities crowd in on us so fast that none of them get the energy they require. Little annoyances can ruin a good part of the day. There comes the day when you arise early to finish paying the bills, get the children off to school, and dress for an important meeting, and then miss the last parking space, which makes you late for work when you cannot spare a moment. Life can seem so full of things that must be done that there is no time merely to relax. Frustration and anxiety set in and we run even faster just to stay in the same place.

Each of us needs rest and quiet for physical and mental health. When we find ourselves constantly rushing to our next task, our minds racing ahead of us, continually feeling under pressure, it is time to stop and assess what is going on. We may find that we are running so hard because we have not found efficient ways of meeting our responsibilities or because we have arranged our lives in order to hide from loneliness or other feelings that could come up in a quiet time. Either way, we can realize that we are endangering our health and well-being by continuing our present course of action.

Reversing a tendency to allow responsibilities to become overwhelming involves, first, arranging for some moments alone with ourselves to find out what is at the basis of the problem. When we take some quiet time, we may find that many feelings come into our awareness. Each one of them is asking to be felt, loved, and understood. The first one is likely to be anger about having so many responsibilities. Next we may feel fear at the prospect of letting go of them even for a short time. By loving these feelings we may, in turn, create room for other feelings to emerge and to be loved. Again, as we allow ourselves to feel, we can learn more about our wants and needs. We may find we need more rest, a solution to a financial problem, a source of sexual satisfaction, a better place to live. Some of our needs may appear to be in conflict with one another. At first we may think that there is no way out, that the only solution is to run harder. This thought is a cue to more feelings that are asking to be integrated. Problems do have solutions, and single people who have taken the risk of giving themselves the gift of feeling and loving their feelings can find the solutions that work best for them.

It can be useful to talk to other single people and to do some reading to find more efficient ways of getting things done. There may be a service available that can clean or do other nitty-gritty tasks that will free one for more important things. Financial advisors are available to help with money concerns. There are career counselors and professional development classes to aid people with work-related issues, and, in fact, there is a resource for help with nearly every kind of need. Health, financial, emotional, child care, and transportation needs are just a few examples. Your public library may have a directory of community services. There are organizations that bring single people together for emotional support, problem solving, and socializing. Perhaps there are some archaic components to your present experience. An experienced therapist may be able to guide you through your resolution of old issues. By thinking about your needs, you will be able to identify the kind of help you may need to meet your responsibilities more effectively.

A primary responsibility of everyone—married or single—is to take time for observing life and integrating feelings. Many learning experiences that arise each day can be overlooked if we do not take time for observation and integration. Life runs more smoothly for people who take time to notice the less obtrusive aspects of existence. If we have lessons to learn in order to become whole, these lessons will be implicit in all of our daily existence. By integrating and understanding small problems now, we may avert larger ones later on. A slight rise in blood pressure may be a signal to ease off a bit in order to avoid health problems later. Small conflicts and discomforts with coworkers may indicate issues that could escalate into business failure unless we allow ourselves the time and space to integrate feelings and understand the source of the problems. Each of us needs a time for renewal and reflection. When we can give ourselves this gift, we will reap the benefits of clearer thought, more effective action, and greater opportunity to actualize our human potential.

Learning from
Our Relationships

Building positive relationships is a major concern for single people. We all need the loving concern and companionship of friends. Most of us wish for the special fulfillment that comes from falling in love and building an intimate relationship. We have sexual needs. We have needs for fun and intellectual stimulation. We may want to have people with whom to share our inner most thoughts and feelings. At one time or another we all wish for attention and for a loving touch. Living seems incomplete without others with whom we can feel close and comfortable.

Our relationships also teach us many things. The people we bring into our lives are mirrors reflecting back to us qualities and needs in ourselves that we might otherwise overlook. A friend may point out a strength that we did not know we had. Someone close to us may share a feeling, and we realize that it is our feeling as well. We may be uncomfortable with someone's attitude and then realize we have the same attitude, perhaps expressed in a different way. When others around us seem unhappy because they are not getting what they want from life, we often find parallels to our own unhappinesses and unmet desires.

We can also learn about what we are not, through our relationships. People close to us may have strengths that we lack but wish to develop in ourselves. They may also have weaknesses that we wish to avoid. Any time we find ourselves experiencing a feeling about the behavior or the words of someone close to us, we have yet another clue to something in ourselves that is asking to be brought into awareness. When we can fully experience our feelings as they arise, we may uncover a strength or a lack that was previously unacknowledged.

The newly single person often finds old friendships no longer satisfying and wishes to develop new relationships. Most of us want both people of the same sex and people of the opposite sex in our lives. The problem becomes how to find the new relationships that will meet our needs. Some people become depressed because they are afraid they will find no one that they can enjoy and love. When you find yourself worred about meeting new people, the time is right to allow yourself to fully experience all of your feelings about being alone, about needing others in your life, and about being afraid that you will not find them. When you have acknowledged and loved your feelings or loved yourself for not loving your feelings, you are in a good position to begin defining what kind of relationships you want and what qualities you are looking for in a friend or a lover.

Clarence was newly divorced. Ever since childhood he had felt uncomfortable with strangers. His father was a military career man. The family had moved often, and Clarence had gone through weeks of agonizing shyness each time he entered a new school. He married a very outgoing young woman and subsequently allowed her to arrange their social life. After the divorce Clarence wanted to be with people but was experiencing a resurgence of the painful shyness he felt as a child.

While Clarence worked on his feelings in therapy, he was asked to make a list of what he wanted in regard to relationships. Here is part of his list:

◻ *I want an exciting sexual relationship.*

◻ *I want a couple of men friends to play tennis with.*

◻ *I want to meet a lot of attractive women.*

◻ *I want people I can have fun with.*

◻ *I want someone who will listen to me and understand me.*

◻ *I don't want women who will lie to me.*

Clarence was then asked to take his list and develop a more precise picture for himself about the qualities and experiences he wanted. He was asked to be totally positive by avoiding the use of the words "no" or "not." He then wrote out exactly what his idea of an exciting relationship experience was. He defined what was attractive to him in a woman and what he meant by having fun. He identified the things about himself that he wanted understood and how he would know when someone listened to him. He defined honesty and fairmindedness in terms of what his needs and wants were. He outlined the skill level and interests of men he would enjoy playing tennis with.

In doing this exercise, Clarence also paid attention to the feelings that came up for him. He let himself be aware of his ambivalence about certain sexual experiences that he wanted to explore. He allowed himself to feel unworthy as he pictured the kind of woman that he wanted to meet. He noticed and integrated his feelings of competitiveness toward his ideal tennis partner.

Clarence was asked to try an experiment the next time he went out for an evening. Before he left his apartment he would picture in his mind precisely what his hopes were for the evening. At the same time he would integrate any feelings his images called out. On his way, and when he reached his destination, he would continue to be aware of his feelings and his wants. Clarence called his counselor on Sunday afternoon. "I tried it and it worked!" he said excitedly. "I was sitting in a bar feeling really uncomfortable and scared about being there alone. So I just let myself feel that way. Suddenly this beautiful woman I'd met once before popped out of the crowd and introduced herself. She told me she'd been wanting to meet me for a long time. We talked for awhile and spent the night at her place. It was unreal. I still can't believe it really happened."

Clarence continued to expand and define his list of wants and needs as he learned more about himself through his experiences. He found that much of what he wanted changed over time and that many feelings needed integration in the process. He learned that he was very capable of meeting people and building relationships to whatever level he desired. As he grew and changed, he found that he grew away from some of the people that had been appropriate friends at certain times. He learned how to say good-bye gently and move on to new experiences.

The newly single person is in a life transition that can bring with it many changes in self-concept and needs. As a result, relationships that fulfill us today may become inappropriate to our continued growth tomorrow. As we change, some people we have been close to may pass out of our lives. Sometimes this happens effortlessly. There are fewer and fewer opportunities to get together, and eventually contact ceases as both people become more involved in other activities. Sometimes, however, we are tied together by strong feelings and common activities to the extent that lessening contact and decreasing emotional involvement is difficult and painful.

At times when it is appropriate to break off or drastically redefine a relationship, it can be most helpful to be clear and honest with the friend. This does not mean providing a rundown of all the faults you see in him or her but, rather, identifying clearly your own needs and wants and explaining why it seems to you that a change is necessary. Once you both have reached an understanding of the situation, you may find ways to help one another over the rough spots that crop up as you disengage.

Martha and Paul had met at a singles club. Both of them were going through painful divorces, and they found the understanding and comfort they needed in one another's company. After a few months Paul moved into Martha's house. He taught her how to repair her car and helped with the heavy chores. She became involved in his business and earned extra money by doing his accounting. The income supplemented her support payments and enabled her to afford some extras for herself and her children. This arrangement was satisfying to both partners for a couple of years.

Eventually Martha realized that her needs and wants in a long-term relationship were very different from Paul's. She kept her feelings to herself for several months because she loved Paul and did not want to hurt him. She saw also that they had come to depend on one another for the smooth functioning of certain aspects of their daily life. In time it became apparent that something had to be done with the situation because tensions and misunderstandings were on the increase between them. Martha no longer was as interested in investing the emotional energy she had previously given to the relationship. Paul was puzzled by the lessened involvement and felt hurt and unvalued.

One weekend Martha explained to Paul what she wanted from a long-term relationship. Paul was honest enough with himself to see that his needs and wants did not correspond very closely with Martha's. At first he was angry at Martha but soon he realized that the most constructive step they could take would be to separate. Paul and Martha shared some very sad hours as they acknowledged the good things they had received from one another and the real love that they shared.

Out of their caring for one another they both wanted to make the separation as easy as possible. Paul's first impulse had been to pack a suitcase and leave immediately. Instead, he and Martha looked together for a new place for him to live. Martha helped him pick out furniture and worked with him on painting and repairing his new home. He, in turn, recommended Martha to one of his business associates who was looking for a part-time bookkeeper. Paul was sure when he said his final goodbys that Martha would be as financially well off without him as she had been with him.

It is seldom easy to say goodby to someone who has been close and important. We can learn to confront our feelings honestly and acknowledge both the positive and the negative in the separation. Often we can find ways of leaving our partner stronger rather than weaker than when we met them. Sadness and loneliness are inevitable companions to the loss of an important relationship. With love for ourselves and one another we may move through the pain to yet another phase of living.

Being single can bring exciting challenges and overwhelming pain into our lives. One of the greatest challenges of singleness is in confronting ourselves. We can learn to grow through our sorrows as well as our joys. Each one of our experiences is an invitation to come closer to ourselves and to know more about who we are. Single people have much freedom to explore themselves as workers, as friends and lovers, and as creative beings. Roles can be tried on, learned from, and discarded without bringing pain and confusion into the lives of others. The freedom in being single has attendant responsibilities. The major responsibility is in using every experience as a vehicle for becoming whole. As we grow toward wholeness we are able to give more to ourselves and to those around us. When we stumble on the journey we may find as we stop to look that the rock that tripped us is actually a diamond of great value.

12

FOR
MEN AND WOMEN
ONLY

It appears that since the dawn of the species, men and women have failed to see eye to eye. Even the earliest literature is full of accounts of misunderstandings and conflict between the sexes. It seems as though we are designed to complement and support one another, yet too often we find ourselves at odds.

Over the last hundred years, women have become more vocal about these problems. Many advances have been made in that time to provide increased equality under the law and greater opportunity for women to express themselves as individuals. However, the battle of the sexes rages on today with more intensity than ever.

What do women want anyway? This question burst from Sigmund Freud toward the end of a lifetime of trying to understand the human mind. The question is still being asked daily in books, magazines, political debates, and private conversations. Answers are given just as often. The fact that this issue is still being discussed so energetically is an indication that the problem is not being solved by the many positive advances that have occurred in the status of women in recent years. The problems that exist between men and women go beyond equal opportunity. It is to our advantage, however, that we are identifying more clearly each day what the problem is not. In this way we are eliminating the barriers to seeing what the real problem is. As a result, we may soon be able to speak to each other clearly across the gulf that has separated us, with the intent and hope that one day we will emerge from the battle with both sexes winners.

Currently a popular component of business and government staff-development programs is the affirmative action workshop. These workshops are designed to enhance understanding between men and women in the working world. Participants are often asked to complete the statement, "Men are . . . ." and "Women are . . . ." several times by using short descriptive words and phrases. The lists often come out looking like the following one:

Men are:	Women are:
strong	*loving*
intelligent	*mothers*
angry	*emotional*
hard workers	*weak*
fixers	*easily upset*
money earners	*confused*
unemotional	*there when you need them*
fun to be with	*good cooks*
powerful	*gentle*

big	*soft and warm*
loud and boisterous	*sneaky*
tough	*pretty*

The facilitator will point out to the class, that, while some of the qualities identified with each sex are positive and others negative, all of the characteristics in both lists are human qualities. Each one of us by virtue of being a member of the human race has within us the potential to be strong *and* weak, tough *and* gentle, good cooks *and* fixers of things. At this point in our evolution, however, we do not have the option to choose freely from among all possible human responses the most appropriate one to any given situation. If a response is not within the sex role that we have been taught from childhood, it is not available to us. Most often we do not even allow ourselves to consider the possibility of feeling or acting in a manner that we consider outside of our male or female role. We are jarred by the sight of a crying man or an angry woman. In fact, no matter how sophisticated we may think we are, we may perhaps wonder for a moment about the person's masculinity or feminity.

Intensified Problems
in Today's Society

The problems between men and women have become more acute in the last decade. That is true, in part, because some of these problems have been recognized, and the few steps that have been taken to rectify inequalities have led to rising expectations of a total resolution. In the past, when men and women met only over the dinner table or in bed it was easier for us to dismiss one another as different and impossible to understand. Today, as we meet more often on the construction site and in the halls of Congress, the distinctions are becoming blurred, and we experience increasing conflict. Even old refuges like the poker game and the hairdresser fail to provide a respite because the major conflict is not between us but within us.

Women were first to begin to reflect seriously on the battlefield within. Someday, perhaps, the greatest impact of the postwar technological revolution will be seen as having come not from the development of the computer and the transistor but from the mass production of labor-saving consumer products such as the automatic dishwasher and permanent press clothing. They created an unprecedented potential for leisure for great numbers of women. Along with increased opportunity for education, volunteer work, and creative homemaking, this new leisure provided many women with the gift of time for introspection. Often this gift was not welcome, for it brought with it an awareness of dissatisfaction. Women began to question the worth of their traditional role within a rapidly changing society. As the rhythms of the outside world increased to a frenzied crescendo, women found their own rhythms to be out of harmony. They experienced a decreasing ability to have an impact on their environment coupled with an increasing sense of helplessness and frustration. Their lives were out of their control, and, with each passing year, that control was becoming more difficult to regain.

However vague and ill-defined this realization was for the individual woman, the internal conflict it generated was difficult to ignore. Solutions were sought. In the 1950s the discomfort was reflected in a rush to the psychiatrist's couch and in such popular cultural trends as the "togetherness" movement and do-it-yourselfism. In the 1960s we saw women becoming increasingly involved in the political process, in work, and in education.

Talking Together
Brings New Awarenesses

During the 1960s we also saw the beginnings of a change in women's relationships with one another. Small groups of women began meeting together regularly but not for the traditional purposes of raising funds for charity or discussing homemaking and child rearing. Women opened up a new topic for discussion, one seldom shared before. The topic was themselves, their own fears and sorrows, their own feelings of incompleteness and unfulfillment. They shared with one another their sense of helplessness when confronted with the world outside their door. Their realization grew that they were dependent on others to repair the machinery that they used each day in their homes. They saw that the money for these repairs and for everything they needed came from the labor of their men. They thought about their own ability to survive and provide for their children if their relationships should end through death or divorce. As they looked at their relationships they grew even more fearful when they recognized that these relationships were primarily held together by convention and social pressures. They wondered what had happened to the love and closeness they had once shared with their men, and they lamented its loss.

One of the greatest things that these women learned by beginning to share their feelings together was that they were not alone. The uneasiness that had seemed an individual weakness in the 1950s was in fact shared by many other women. Not only that, there also seemed to be some real reasons for these feelings. As they looked around them they could find few women who were able to command salaries equal to men. They identified legal and social barriers that impeded the efforts of single women to survive in everyday life. They saw how the pressures on women to find and hold a man interfered with the equal give and take that is essential to intimacy in a relationship. The clearer they became about their relationships with the world, the more their fear escalated. It seemed as if they were truly helpless and that under such conditions personal security was a myth for women.

For many women the situation was intolerable. There had to be a solution and, under the circumstances, the solution seemed clear. If we feel and are helpless, the women reasoned, then we must become powerful. The decision was made, and in the making of it, women let go of the close contact they were feeling with their fear.

It seemed to these women that the power they needed lay in the world of men. Men controlled the political and economic establishment and were resistant to allowing women full partnership within their territory. Boardrooms and bars were off limits to women who asked to be included. It looked as if the men derived security from their place within the establishment. It was at this point that the women's fear began to generate anger. The issues were ones of survival in the world. Women perceived men as standing in the way of their survival, and they grew angry.

The feminist movement of the sixties and seventies was born out of the fear of helplessness, the desire to gain personal security, and the anger that arose out of fear when it seemed as if men were creating barriers to women's achievement of their goals. From the beginning, the movement has been plagued by internal disagreement. One branch of the movement is committed to achieving partnership for women within the established power structure, the other aims to tear down this structure and create a new egalitarian and humanitarian society. Among the problems with both of these solutions is the fact that women are not aware that the men's ostensible ability to control their own destiny through the political and economic power structure is not, in fact, a reality.

The masculine sex role dictates that a man must be powerful. He must think and act assertively in order to be in control of the world around him. By definition, any male who does not live up to this role and who is not in charge at all times is not truly a man. In reality, this image is more often wishful thinking than actuality, as we shall see. Women, by asking for partnership with men, have created a threat that goes far beyond what is commonly supposed. Men are not being threatened by a loss or dilution of power but with exposure to the inner realization that the power and control they believe they must have to be real men does not exist.

Women's new awareness and the resultant resistance to the new energy they have generated to create a change has brought about a wide-ranging and powerful social controversy. In the hopes of regaining control over their own lives, many women have banded together to win public office for women, to lobby for equal rights legislation, and to achieve financial self-determinism. Other women have joined together to oppose these aims. Antifeminist women's groups gain their impetus from the same realization of helplessness. The women in these groups experience as much personal insecurity, but their own fear and their analysis of the situation has brought them to an entirely different conclusion. To them, a return to the old ways seems preferable to stepping into new roles. Both sides expend huge quantities of energy in rhetoric and action aimed at subduing what is perceived as a threat to each individual's survival.

The Root
of the Conflict

In order to begin to see our way out of this conflict, it is necessary to recognize the feelings that are at its root. It is the fear of helplessness and the sense of loss of control of our own destinies that gives impetus to the anger we direct toward each other, to the millions of written and spoken words defining the roles of women today, and to the countless hours of labor based on the various opinions of how to solve the problem.

It is not the authors' intent to propose yet another scenario for an ideal world of peace and equality. Rather, it is our intent to point out some aspects of the problem that have perhaps been overlooked, so that we can come to terms with our own femaleness and maleness and claim our personhood.

There is nothing intrinsically wrong with marriage or singleness, with a career- or a home-centered life. Today women have more appropriate and viable alternatives than ever before. As we have seen earlier, it is our beliefs and opinions about what is correct or acceptable that are the main barriers that keep us from seeing clearly all possibilities and aspects of a situation. Any of a myriad of alternatives may fit for a given woman at any stage in her growth and development. Reducing these alternatives from the level of choice to the level of right and wrong may result in creating new stereotypes, more "shoulds" and "oughts" that will further imprison women and slow their development. Women can find the security they need. It will come out of knowing themselves and being who they really are, not by living up to some image or stereotype. Each time we truly know ourselves, we enhance our security, and we find there is something new to learn. By taking the time to acknowledge and to feel the fears and angers that are with us now, and by learning to love ourselves for being exactly who we are at any given moment, we will become calm and clear enough to create solutions that are real rather than illusory. Our solutions then may be just the same as they are now. It is also possible that they will be very different. The big difference, however, will be that they are *our* solutions, which will serve us without harming others.

For many women, reaching the goal of obtaining the personal security that arises from within will be a result of the process of effectively confronting the problems that arise in everyday life. The authors have discussed a number of living problems shared by many of us. What can be shared here is the possibility open to each woman of regaining the sense of who she is and what she needs at each moment of her life.

A woman's major strength lies in her ability to be close to her feelings. Many women have cut themselves off from an awareness of their own feelings because those feelings have seemed inappropriate or ineffective. When women can return to their inner experience, they will begin to establish a more secure connection with the outside world. This connection will be more real and valid because it will arise from the inner core.

There is plenty of evidence to support the reality that women are able to learn the skills necessary to achieve and survive in the world. Women are learning to repair their own machinery. Women have gone back to school. They have won political office. Any woman can find the role that fits comfortably for her when she allows herself to feel the feelings that are messages from her inner self about who she really is. Once felt, these feelings need to be loved. The woman who fears her inadequacy may find that by loving these feelings she can go beyond her tenseness and unhappiness to a way of gaining the knowledge she needs to become more effective. Each moment, she can learn to be aware of the feelings she is experiencing as she goes about her daily life. Little by little she will recognize how she helps herself and where she is working against herself. With this recognition, and with love for herself, she can begin to uncover the inner and outer resources she needs to enable herself to grow gently into the person she wishes to be.

One of the authors was privileged to be able to share a part of this process with Ginnie, a woman who for many years had felt overshadowed by her outstandingly creative and successful husband. Ginnie joined an assertiveness training group because she felt unable to maintain her own self-worth in the face of what seemed to be the overwhelming success of her husband. During the eight weeks that the group met together, Ginnie found the listening ears that she had been seeking. She shared her fears, frustration, and helplessness. In addition to giving the empathic understanding that allowed Ginnie to really feel her pent-up feelings, the group also gave her their opinions. They did not see her as helpless at all. Again and again, group members pointed out her strengths and accomplishments and affirmed their value. At the final group meeting, Ginnie announced her plans to attend law school. Her desire for a legal career had been put on the shelf years before at the time of her marriage. Ginnie is now in her third year of studying law and is in the top half of her class. She keeps in touch and says that, while she is enjoying learning the law, the best thing about her life right now is how much she is learning about herself.

Men Have Problems Too

Men play the flip side of the sex-role stereotype. They are trained from childhood to think and act. They are required to make decisions, to solve problems, and to control the world around them. They are asked to be pillars of strength, to know what to do in difficult situations. They must have the answer, and they must have it fast. Not only that, but the answer must be the right one. Men are always busy and constantly have important matters on their minds. It is on their shoulders that the national security and the rent payment rest. Men are respected, recognized, and deferred to. Their achievements are written up in newspapers and national magazines. We see them at work on the nightly news. A man, if he is successful, is constantly challenging the limits of human achievement. Men will set the new track record, develop the new product, conceive the idea that solves the knotty problem.

Men are not only given the opportunity—they are required—to perform and achieve to the maximum of their ability. For a man, life should be an endless exploration of new frontiers. There are always new worlds to be won. These expectations can result in an infinitely exciting existence. Excitement, however, is first cousin to anxiety. Stress-related diseases are an occupational hazard of being male. The male population of the United States is plagued by a high incidence of impotence, ulcers, heart disease, circulatory problems, and untimely death.

More difficult to measure but no less real are the problems men experience in sustaining close interpersonal relationships. Their marriages disintegrate before their eyes. Their children rebel against them and the values that they have built their lives upon. Few men can name even one male with whom they can honestly share their inner experience. Some men do find it possible to share something of themselves with a woman. Often the woman a man chooses to receive his confidences is one whose existence in his life is a secret to his family and friends. Her position in his life prevents the development of true intimacy between them.

Competition is the keystone of living for men. At work and at play he is judged on the basis of his wins and losses. He has the freedom only to choose the arena within which the judgment will be made. If he chooses the intellectual life, he will be judged by the number and success of his books and lectures. In business, the judgment will concern itself with his ability to make money and amass material goods. In politics the standard is power. In sports it is skill and records set. In relationships it may be the number of sexual conquests or the longevity of his erection. It is not just others who will assess his worth in this manner. He himself will constantly measure his own progress and inevitably find that someone else is doing better.

The competition grows fierce as the amount of information available to us about the world we live in increases, far beyond the ability of anyone of us to absorb and handle. Each day countless men accomplish twice as much as should be reasonably expected of any human being, and they return again the next day to do the same. The harder they run, the more aware they become of falling behind. As we increase our efforts to gain control of the external world, our sense of failure and frustration mounts. Our world today has a momentum of its own that is far beyond the ability of one person or one group of people to affect in any significant way.

The problem for men is, then, that in order to fulfill their sex role they must be strong, powerful, and able to control their environment effectively. This being an impossible task, the next best thing is to perform in such a way as to appear to be in control in the hopes that someday the impossible may actually be achieved. As we have seen, it is more likely that the achievement will be a diseased body or a disastrous personal life.

For men as well as for women the fear of helplessness, the vague sense of personal insecurity, is at the root of many of life's difficulties. In many ways the problem may be more intense for men. Although men's greatest strengths may be in their ability to think and do, their emphasis on the manipulation and control of the exterior has created a complementary atrophy of awareness of the interior. Men have not been encouraged to feel their feelings and have therefore lost the awareness of the many feelings that normally would arise in the course of a day. Only the most intense of these feelings such as anger and sexual excitement, can force themselves through the physical and mental barriers with any regularity. Even those are often perceived as inappropriate and are therefore suppressed or ignored. Because only very strong pent-up feelings are perceived, feelings themselves are thought of as dangerous and overwhelming. As the pressure of pent-up feelings increases, more and more self-control must be exercised over the years, until something inevitably snaps.

Mike made his first appointment with a therapist because of his suicidal fantasies. His business had recently gone bankrupt, his girl friend had left him for another man, and his health was impaired as a result of excessive alcohol intake. None of this concerned him greatly, however, since he had been in such straits several times before and had always been able to "pull himself up by his bootstraps." Mike's real problem was that his self-control was gone. He found himself breaking into tears at unlikely times. Whenever he was alone, he became overwhelmed by anxiety. He played the radio and TV in order to get to sleep, and he was plagued by insomnia.

Mike feared his inability to control his feelings more than anything else. He had decided to turn off his feelings at an early age, and his decision was reinforced by the anger that broke through his barriers periodically. He was a fighter, and left physical injury and destroyed property in his wake. When he was calm, he criticized himself sharply for his outbreaks of anger and vowed repeatedly never to allow himself to do such a thing again.

He was unaware that the very feelings he wished to control were his major strength in solving the problems that had brought on the depression and anxiety. Slowly he learned that it was his emotional control, the coolness he prided himself on, that sent women away in frustration, realizing that they could never touch him. He grew to understand that his inability to trust his gut reactions to people prevented him from seeing the difference between a smooth manipulator and a trustworthy person. Finally, he realized that the impossible stresses he placed on himself through overwork and the denial of his feelings created an anxiety that only alcohol could anesthetize for a short time. His fear of becoming aware of his inner self caused him to pull away from close relationships and created a gnawing question regarding his own self-worth that more and more success could only temporarily assuage.

Mike decided to bring his feelings back into his life. As he put it, "I know that when members of a work team aren't listened to, they find ways to upset the project. I guess it's the same with my internal team. If I forget to listen to part of myself, that part will throw a monkey wrench into the works."

As a result of his new awareness, Mike decided to change careers. His new work is a nine-to-five job, with no evenings scheduled for catch up or plotting new strategies to put him one ahead of competitors. He makes about as much money as he did before, but spends less on alcohol and more on things he needs for his own growth and development. He is developing a relationship with a woman who understands his fears about himself, and he is learning little by little to open his deeper heart.

Mike's case shows us that unresolved or unrecognized feelings support invalid thoughts and opinions. Judgment is clouded when feelings are not taken into account, and decisions and actions are often inappropriate to the present situation. Thought and action can be accurate only when all factors are taken into account. Feelings exist in all of us. They are incontestably a part of human nature. Decisions made in ignorance of the emotional components of the situation will always be ineffective to one degree or another.

Until the feeling component of man's being is acknowledged and integrated, the fear of failure will be a very realistic one, because failure will be inevitable. For men as well as for women, the way out, as always, is *through*. Men can reestablish a connection with the inner core of their experience. The world cannot be controlled by force of will. It can, however, be related to harmoniously by the individual who is at one with himself. There will still be new worlds to explore and problems to be solved. Actions taken from a position of inner peace and harmony result in real solutions, solutions that do not create several additional problems for every problem solved.

For the man who chooses to begin to change his life around and recontact the part of himself that he has forgotten, the only place to start is where he is. If he is unaware of the messages his body is sending him, he can stop and listen. If he finds to his dismay that the first thing he learns about himself is that he is full of fear and anger, then he can call on his ability to care about himself and to admit those feelings into his awareness. He can learn the skill of loving himself for having his feelings. Finally, he can develop the understanding of how he has brought those feelings into his life and determine whether or not he is willing to continue to live with the problems he is creating.

Men and women have much to learn from one another. Each of us needs the part of himself or herself that is the strength of the other. The problems that we experience as men and women living in today's world may be just the gift that we need to enable us to find a part of ourselves that we have lost and, in the process of rediscovery, to become whole. The time to begin is any time that we wish.

13

ENLIGHTENMENT
AND
BEYOND

This chapter can serve as a lazy way to remember all the information we have discussed up until now; plus, as a bonus, it describes some further awarenesses.

Enlightenment is a process of getting it and losing it, doing it and not doing it, feeling and not feeling, making your life work and forgetting how to make it work. Enlightenment is not a place you get to, it's a way of getting places. And this chapter might be useful in turning things around when you're heading in the wrong direction, remembering when you're heavily into forgetting.

Enlightenment comes in stages. First, there's *Little E.*

Little E is experiences in personal harmony. Little E is becoming aware of something, experiencing it, loving it, figuring out what you want, then forgetting to do all those good things, then remembering again. Little E is remembering to ask yourself when you're feeling stuck:

◻ *What is it I'm not willing to look at right now?*

◻ *What is it I'm not willing to experience right now?*

◻ *Is it fear?*

◻ *Is it anger?*

◻ *Is it my sexual feelings?*

◻ *Is it hurt or sadness?*

Remember: what we are unwilling to experience runs us. Little E is remembering to ask yourself:

◻ *What do I want right now?*

◻ *Love?*

◻ *Attention?*

◻ *Something in the material world?*

◻ *Nurturing?*

◻ *What am I resisting loving in myself?*

There are many things about ourselves we do not love.

◻ *anger*

◻ *fear*

◻ *sexual feelings*

◻ *wants and desires*

◻ *our bodies*

You can start by loving yourself for not loving those parts of you. Then you can love each of those parts of you. Say hello to something you do not like about yourself. Love it for a second, then let it go. You can even love yourself for hating yourself. And love yourself for reading this sentence. Love all your reactions to things.

Remember, love starts at home —inside. Then, when you've loved yourself a little, you open up space to love others. Loving others without loving yourself really well first is a drain and doesn't work very well. If you'd like to kill some part of yourself, love it to death. Love as much of yourself as you can from where you stand. If you'd like to kill someone, love your anger, then love that person to death. Remember, too, that you can have everything you need. To get what you want:

¤ *Give yourself permission to want it.*

¤ *Let yourself feel your want down deep.*

¤ *Love yourself for wanting it.*

¤ *Let it go.*

It'll come to you if it's something that would be of service to your evolution. Then, when you get good at experiencing yourself

¤ *loving your body*

¤ *and your feelings*

¤ *and your wants and needs*

you can realize that you *are* the universe. It's not you versus it. *You are it.* And so are your friends, your neighbors, the people you hate, the plants in your garden, the cars on the highway. It is all you, and you are all it. You are the universe

◻ *reading a sentence about itself*

◻ *wondering, beginning to understand itself*

◻ *looking around and seeing itself*

This is *Big E.* With your personal harmony growing, and your relationship with the universe secure, you can do anything you want, be any way you need to be. And it's all right, because everywhere you go is home.

And when you come back from Big E and find you're home, which of course is now everywhere, one thing you'll want to do is straighten things up a little. You can do this not with a heavy attitude of, "I've got to look out for everybody else," but with the light air of knowing that we're all one, that one of the things you can do as a representative of the universe is to extend a loving hand to another representative, whether that representative be a child, an enemy, or a tomato plant. Then you can be the universe embracing itself, then reaching out to embrace more of itself. With loving arms outstretched to embrace yourself, to embrace others around you and the universe itself, you become the universe loving itself. What better thing can there be?